PRAISE FOR

When Words Don't Come Easy

"My heart is so deeply stirred by this powerful book! *When Words Don't Come Easy*, by my dear friend Andy Howard, is a message of hope, freedom, redemption, and purpose. I know the man, I know the message, and they align. Andy and I have traveled the globe together, and I have seen how God uses him to be a messenger of hope to thousands. Andy has personally brought hope to me on so many occasions. He has the ability to awaken people out of defeat and into purpose and victory. *When Words Don't Come Easy* will be a healing balm for the soul. Andy and his book exemplify the simple verse found in Isaiah 26:3, 'You will keep in perfect peace those whose minds are steadfast, because they trust in you.'"

Pat Schatzline

Evangelist, Author, & CEO
Remnant Ministries International & Two Crazy Dreamers, LLC

"Grab a box of tissues (trust me, you'll need it) to wipe your tears from both crying and laughing, and settle down in your favorite chair to read this powerful book. Prepare yourself to be impacted by Andy's journey. Allow him to run his fingers through your wounds and run yours through his. If you can do this, I believe you will experience the healing and freedom you've been contending for in your life!"

Leanne Goff

Author & President and Founder of Leanne Goff Ministries

"Wow! This book left me wrecked (in a really good way) and overflowing with hope at the same time. *When Words Don't Come Easy* is a great reminder of the goodness of God, even when we don't understand why things happen the way they do. What an incredible exclamation point on the fact that life doesn't happen to us, but happens for us if we trust God and allow Him to do what he does best: redeem!"

Dan Valentine

CEO, Valentine Health LLC

"Andy Howard's book is heartbreaking, inspiring, and instructive. His transparency will encourage you to face the crippling self-doubt so many of us have suffered with. But this is not simply a story of past pain now overcome; it is a testament to how present pain doesn't need to keep us from an overcoming life. Thank you, Andy, for sharing it with us."

Dave Olson

Lead Pastor, Heartland Church in Ankeny, Iowa

"Raw, authentic, inspiring, healing. These are the words that come to mind when reading Andy Howard's book, When Words Don't Come Easy. Life can seem unfair at times and there are struggles that go so deep you don't want anyone to know. But Andy pulls back the covers of shame and guilt and shows the path to freedom. Get ready to breakthrough fear, depression, or anything holding you back. God is for you and will be faithful to bring you through!"

Matt Sorger

Author & Founder of Sorger Ministries International and Rescue1

"There are helpful books—and then there are transformative books. When Words Don't Come Easy is the latter. Andy Howard unflinchingly shares the most difficult moments of his life to offer real hope in our darkest days. If you need hope, you'll find it here. If you need inspiration, you'll find it here. If you want a better life, you'll find the keys in these pages."

Jordan Loftis

Bestselling Author, Speaker, & President and
Editor of Short Daily Devotions

There is beauty in the broken

WHEN
WORDS DON'T
COME EASY

How God Redeems Our Stories,
Gives Purpose to Our Pain,
and Still Uses Us to Change the World

ANDY HOWARD

WHEN WORDS DON'T COME EASY

Published by

STORY ᏊᏊ CHORUS

Learn more at StoryChorus.com

Dedication

To Tiffany, Baby P, Park, and Pres,
There's no one else I would rather be on this journey with than all of you.
May we always find the beauty in the broken.

Contents

Foreword

Where to begin? I have put off writing this foreword for a while. Yes, those who know me may know I procrastinate at times, but the reason I've put this off is simple: I don't even know how to put into words my excitement for you to read this book. It's been a long time coming. And it means so much to me for you to hear this incredible story of hope because I know the power of Jesus in these stories. I just want to give it the justice it deserves.

Let me first give you a little behind-the-scenes on the author. Doesn't everyone like that good behind-the-scenes footage? It's my favorite part at the end of some movies. See, Andy is the love of my life. Twenty-three years ago, I knew without a shadow of a doubt the Lord sent him to me to save me from myself. I was heading down a dark path. I was young and buying into the lies of the world. In a series of events only Jesus can orchestrate, Andy showed up on the scene; and from that moment forward, everything in my life changed. For the better. I had no idea the pain and heartache that laid ahead; but Jesus did, and he sent Andy to walk it all out with me, hand in hand.

Outside of Jesus, Andy is my hero. Yeah, it sounds sappy, but it's true. I serve the Lord today because of Andy's unashamed walk with Christ at such a young age. When everyone else was trying to fit in, Andy was an unapologetic Christian deeply rooted in his faith and relationship with Christ. Even as I write this, the memories come flooding back from when we met, and I am overwhelmed with thankfulness and respect for him.

I know people can lie on social media and show you the highlight reel of their lives. I know we live in a day and age where people are really good at fooling others into making them see only what they want them to see. But I've walked this life with Andy day in and day out for the last twenty-three years. Andy is the most Godly man I know. He has more character and integrity than any person I've ever met. He is kind and compassionate. He is beyond humble. He has a servant's heart and always puts everyone's needs and desires above his own. He is everything I hope to be, and he challenges me in my faith walk just through his everyday life.

I share all this with you so you can know the person behind the pen. Andy has been called to write a book for over ten years. As you'll see in the upcoming chapters, he let fear hold him back for a long time. The enemy is really good at silencing those who would bring hope and impact to the world.

I couldn't be any prouder or more thankful that he finally pushed that fear aside as I *know* the book you hold in your hands will bring you hope. This book is extremely relevant to the days we are living in. Suicide is at an all-time high. Depression is rampant in our world. Currently, I believe it's the greatest tactic the enemy is using. I personally grew up in a culture where if you struggled with depression, you must not be a strong enough Christian, or not pray hard enough, or not trust God enough, or (fill in the blank). I believed that lie for years. Maybe you have, too. But depression is no respecter of persons, and as you'll see in the upcoming chapters, even a pastor who has dedicated his entire life to the ministry and calling of God can be chased down and held captive by depression.

My prayer is that as you read these pages, Jesus—His hope, love, and freedom—will begin to make Himself known to you. I have no doubt He will. Although I lived so many of these stories, I can't begin to tell you what it was like reading them through Andy's eyes. Each chapter had me laughing hysterically and bawling like a baby. I may be biased, but it's really, really good, y'all. After finishing the book myself, I realize why the devil tried so hard to convince Andy not to write it for these past ten years. Get ready, my friends. I pray you read this with your heart wide open. Jesus is ready to fill it and set you free.

Andy, there aren't words to say how proud of you I am. You are my hero. I've never respected another human as much as I respect you. I have no idea why God saw fit to give you to such a mess as me, but I will forever be thankful He did. You are the best husband and father anyone could ask for. All those years ago, I would have never thought someone like you existed. Thank you for loving me through my own depression. Thank you for being the beacon of hope for me. Thank you for modeling Jesus to our family. Thank you for being there for me when times got so, so tough. You've been my steady rock. My calm in the storms. I don't think I would have lived through this story had it not been for you, your strength, and your unwavering faith in Jesus. Thank you for writing this book. Thank you for being willing to share all the really hard things, and so authentically. When others may have chosen to hide the pain, you put it all out there in the hope of impacting just one life for the better. I have no doubt one day we'll cross into eternity and get to see thousands of lives radically impacted by this book.

Love, your biggest fan,

Tiffany

Let's Have Coffee?

Whoever you are, and however you got your hands on this book, thank you. Let's start with something cool: I've been praying for you. Why? Because I don't believe in accidents.

You're holding this book for a reason. Maybe a friend gifted you a copy, or you picked it up at your neighbor's garage sale for a quarter. No matter how this book found its way to you, I'm so glad it did. Because this just might be a moment where the Great "I AM" (who I partnered with daily to get this project done) wakes something inside you.

I remember the moment that happened to me when I was a 17-year-old junior in high school. A rockstar speaker, Reggie Dabbs, brought the house down at a youth convention in Dallas, Texas with a powerful message. The funny thing is, I remember almost everything about that day—down to the bright red boxing gloves he used as a sermon illustration. Everything except what he said during his message.

What hit me came at the end. He invited the crowd of thousands of kids to a different kind of altar call. His voice blared over the speakers, "I want the ones who are called to ministry *and* willing to serve to join me at the front."

My heart just about pounded out of my chest. It was like everything in my life had led me to this moment—and I ran to the altar at the front of the auditorium. I made a promise to God that day that I would immediately say, "Yes!" every time He opened a door for me to speak and share some hope with a hurting world.

I do not take that moment lightly. Because that's the day I met my purpose. And this book is just another way for me to say "Yes!" to God. No matter where you're at in your life—whether you feel busted up, beyond repair, or just too tired to carry on—I have a story about broken things becoming beautiful ... about hopeless situations turning into victory beyond imagination ... and ink-black nights of depression giving way to light.

It's not a story of shortcuts or easy ways out of pain. Instead, it's about the guts of what can happen even when you're walking through valleys too deep to see the sky. It's my story. The good, the bad, and the ugly.

If you're hurting, I wrote this for *you.*

If you're at the end of your rope, I wrote this for *you.*

If you don't know how the mortgage is gonna get paid next month, I wrote this for *you.*

I want you to know that there is hope on the other side of pain. I experienced this on one of the worst days of my life (and trust me, *that* is saying something). But before I get any further, I have to tell you about a kid named Jonathan whose story inspired me to write this book in the first place.

In the 1970s, Jonathan was a struggling musician who had big dreams and empty pockets. He was scraping pennies together to get by, taking every gig he could get. About the only thing he had going for him was a friend who never left his side, his dog. Then, one day, with the rent due and only barely having the money to pay it, Jonathan's dog got hit by a car. The vet saved his life, but Jonathan left with a hurting puppy and a $900 bill he didn't have the cash for.

Embarrassed and thoroughly humbled, he called his dad to ask for *yet another* loan. He asked, "Dad, am I just dreaming? Should I just come back home to Chicago?"

His dad replied, "I'll give you the loan, but you gotta stay put." Then, after a beat of silence, he said the magic words: "Son, don't stop believin'."

That kid was Jonathan Cain. He wrote the lyrics to "Don't Stop Believin'" after that conversation with his dad. Then, in 1980, a little band you may have heard of called Journey asked him to join. One day, their legendary frontman Steve Perry told him they needed another song for their album, *Escape*. Steve asked if Jonathan had any ideas.

Jonathan flipped through his notebook and found two lines: "Don't stop believin', hold on to that feeling." He took them back to the studio, and the rest is history.

His story, and that song, are so fitting for this book. Honestly, I've known for more than a decade that I was supposed to write this book. No joke. But every time I decided to start writing, I found five reasons to stop. Now, though, you and I are meeting in what I believe is God's perfect timing.

So, read this book as if we were sitting across the table at your favorite coffee shop, having a cup, and going deep. OK, fine . . . I'd order a double shot of espresso, a glass of iced tea, and talk way too fast—but let's not get lost in the weeds. Grab a cup of your favorite beverage, and let's have a conversation about hope. For you. For me. And for everyone you meet.

Now, let me share my story to help you find yours. For me, it all began with a question: What's on the other side of fear? The answer changed everything.

CHAPTER 1

The Other Side of Fear

You have a story. So do I. Every one of us was created with a powerful story to live and share. But for one reason or another, we choose to remain silent. That's the safe option. If we don't share it, we can't be criticized. No one will question your story . . . No one will laugh at you . . . No one will tell you what you should have done differently. By keeping quiet, we don't have to face our fears of other peoples' uncomfortable (and usually unwelcome) opinions. You know, the ones that hurt us and often make our pain, shame, or embarrassment even worse.

Silent equals safe as a turtle in its shell. It protects us from rejection—one of our deepest fears. Biologically, this makes total sense. Did you know that scientists have discovered that our brain treats a broken heart just like a broken leg?[1] Rejection is scary. So why ruffle feathers?

Instead, we can keep our heads buried in the sand. All the while, we hope for change in a thousand different ways but do absolutely nothing to stir the waters around us. Let me ask you a hard question I have to answer myself every day: how can you move forward in life if you keep standing still?

What if you changed your perspective with me—just for a second? And instead of focusing on the criticism and judgment you and I are both so afraid of, we imagine what's on the other side of fear? Would you dare go there with me?

---

1   Kirsten Weir, *"The pain of social rejection,"* Monitor on Psychology 43, *no. 4 (April 2012): 50, https://www.apa.org/monitor/2012/04/rejection.*

It's all about perception. When viewed from one side, it looks big and hairy and terrifying like the monster under the bed. But what if there's something more wonderful, beautiful, and brighter than you ever thought possible waiting on the other side of that fear? Because remember, even though the monster under our beds or in our closets as kids was only a figment of our imagination, so is the fear keeping us quiet. It's all bark, no bite.

For whatever reason, it's been a while since you tasted victory. So, failing or feeling small has become second nature, and we anticipate negative outcomes. How do I know what this feels like? Because I lived there for most of my life. If you're looking for a way past being stuck or a cure for fear, this chapter is for you. And it's really where my personal journey of radical transformation begins—by taking a peek through the keyhole of a very scary door called fear. Let me tell you what I found on the other side.

It's Not About Me (or You)

In John 10:10a, Jesus gave us Satan's war strategy: "The thief comes only to steal and kill and destroy." Stealing, killing, and destroying is scary stuff, right? Maybe if we just stay quiet, we won't draw any unwanted attention from this thief on a warpath against our souls. But I started to see things in a different light when someone told me, "Andy, if you keep playing small, Satan doesn't have to mess with you at all. You're paralyzed with fear and keeping yourself quiet. So why does he have to do anything to keep you quiet? You're doing a really good job of that on your own."

That hurt. But it was true. Is it true for you, too? Does that sound like freedom? Or look like the abundant "life to the fullest" Jesus promised in the rest of John 10:10? Not really! I took this lesson to heart. I embraced my freedom. I accepted the abundant life. And that's all you have to do, right? You just say, "Yeah, Jesus, I want that!" Snap your fingers. And then magically, you're never afraid again. Unfortunately, it doesn't work like that.

On April 28, 2019, I was sitting in my mancave[2] watching my friend Pat Schatzline preach an *amazing* sermon on Facebook Live. I remember the

---

2   *Yes, I have a mancave! I'm a girl-dad of three beautiful daughters and proud of it. I have a drop-dead gorgeous wife. And shoot, even my dog and cat are females. I'm surrounded! Not to mention, we have five nurses who help care for our oldest daughter. They are basically family—and, yes, are also females. So sometimes, a mancave is essential to sanity :).*

date because I've kept the text thread where I told him thank you for three years (as of writing this). I needed that message so badly. I was beaten up and broken down. If life was a race, I felt like I was in last place. But I believe there's always hope for the underdog. As I shared my reality with him, he replied: "Thanks so much for being authentic. It's time to awaken the anointing once again. I believe in you."

He probably has no idea what that meant to me. (So Pat, if you're reading this, *thank you*.) That message of hope was a lifeline tossed to a guy flailing in the middle of the ocean. It tugged me back into the boat and changed the trajectory of where I was headed. It exchanged my defeated outlook for one of victory.

Around the same time, I had another life-altering conversation with a dear friend named JM. I'd confided in him about being nervous for an upcoming talk I had to give. I was going on a missions trip with the aforementioned Pat to South Africa. In all honesty, I was terrified that I was about to screw this up and be a bad representation of his ministry. But instead of saying, "Wow, Andy, I understand. Your life is hard. That's a big responsibility," JM said this: "Bro, it's not about you! The message you're supposed to deliver isn't for *you*, it's for *them*.

Me and my good buddy JM.

Once you really understand that, the pressure is off. You can walk in the Lord's confidence because He's using you to set people free."

Yep. That snapped me out of it. I was spiraling because my focus wasn't on the vision God was calling me to chase—it was on me because I had made everything about me. JM challenged me to "do it scared." So I did. I went to South Africa. I gave the talk. It impacted people in a way I never could have on my own. But guess what? Even after that experience, I'm imperfect. I'm still tempted to give in to fear.

Writing this book has been tremendously difficult. My mind is amazing at crafting excuse after excuse for why I shouldn't share my story with you. However, I've tasted what's on the other side of fear—and it is unbelievably good.

Walking in God's favor is infinitely better than playing it safe. Safe is dangerous when it comes to chasing God's best because you make your impact on the adventure, not on the couch. My story is my story—and I pray it blesses you and everyone else who hears it. Even if no one gets a thing from it, I would still walk in obedience as God called me to share it. It's been a long journey but a fun ride. Through it all, a phrase has been etched into my heart forever: "There is beauty in the broken."

So even as I found myself in a dark place texting my friend Pat . . . Even when my knees were shaking with fear as I talked with JM . . . Even though my fingers don't want to write . . . I've learned that God makes broken, busted, and bruised things beautiful. And that's not just the story of my life, it's the story of everyone's life. You face hardships. You're up against scary things. You have a battle to fight. But no matter how hard, scary, or tough the road ahead is, I promise there is beauty on the other side of fear.

I'm writing this as I prepare to run my second Spartan Race. I remember running my first one a year ago. I was nervous. I'd seen all the YouTube videos of people tripping in the mud, falling over obstacles, and messing up their javelin toss. Did I train enough? Was I strong enough? Did I have the endurance?

On that course, I couldn't help but see my life experience reflected in every obstacle. Climbing over walls and crawling beneath barbed wire perfectly illustrated what Tiffany, my wife, and I have gone through together. But as I ran and climbed and crawled, I looked up from the obstacles. I stopped focusing on the burn in my legs or the gash on my shin. And I looked around at the amazing, wonderful, beautiful friends God had blessed us with.

I wasn't alone.

I'd signed up for this ahead of my 40th birthday because I wanted to do something hard that I'd never done before. And voilà, Spartan Race it was! I didn't want to chicken out, so I invited a bunch of friends to join me for accountability, motivation, and of course, celebration when we were done.

The Spartan is tough, man. They have designed it for one reason only: to get in your head and make you quit. While you need to train your body, it's more about strengthening your mind. As former Dallas Cowboys coach

*Walking in God's favor
is infinitely better
than playing it safe.*

and Hall of Famer Jimmy Johnson said, "Let the mind control the body, not the body control the mind. That is toughness."

Right off the starting line, you're plunged into freezing water with a pack of over one hundred other people. It's a scrum of scrambling racers and ice-cold water that shocks your body. Every cell in my body yelled: "Andy, why are you doing this?! Get out!"

Your body wants to quit—your mind says no. Keep going.

Then you hit the mud and crawl. Like the water, it's frigid. Only it cakes onto you, gets mushed into your mouth, and seeps in between your toes. Once you stagger to your feet, 90 percent of the course stretches out in front of you—usually uphill. Every obstacle thereafter brings new challenges, and your body keeps begging you to quit already.

You might be wondering, what does a Spartan Race have to do with me? If you've been afraid to do something because you might not measure up, then it has *everything* to do with you.

At one point in my life, I weighed 345 pounds. And since I'm not eight feet tall, that was far too heavy. I was so overweight that I actually spent more time looking for a close parking spot at the grocery store or mall than I did shopping. Just walking into the store left me out of breath with a light sweat covering my body. Ugh. I was so unhealthy. I was so sick. I was in pain. And at the race, that 345-pound guy was still somewhere inside of me.

I was terrified to run the Spartan Race with people half my age. But that was when the other-side-of-fear mentality kicked in. *How cool would it feel to finish a Spartan Race at forty years old?* I imagined my wife's smile getting bigger with every mile and obstacle I conquered. The only thing that got me to the starting line was a vision for what could be if I just did it afraid. And I can tell you honestly, crossing the finish line was one of the most exhilarating feelings of my life. It wasn't just good—it was flipping amazing. It was better than I even imagined.

Crossing that finish line represented much more than finishing a hard race. It symbolized a shift in my mindset. Something changed inside of me. Covered in mud, sweat, and a little bit of blood (it was mine, don't worry), I found a new perspective. A new confidence. Each obstacle had been a test—and I passed. This was a big deal because there are many obstacles Tiff and I have faced in life that we weren't sure we could overcome.

As they say in one of our favorite movies, we've been through "a whole heap together."

A Whole Heap

A big question mark hung over my head. That question was whether my future would be filled with toy trucks or dolls, building blocks or princess dresses, league baseball games or father-daughter dances. I was at my day job, trying to get my work done and doing a terrible job of it. My wife and I had a doctor's appointment that day to discover the sex of our child.

Frankly, I had no idea what to do with a daughter. I didn't know girls. I knew boys because I grew up with four older brothers, and I dreamed of things like teaching my son how to do Dirk Nowitzki's legendary one-legged fade-away jump shot or Hakeem Olajuwon's dream shake. And then I daydreamed about more serious things, maybe having to teach him about cars and his wedding day—I'd almost imagined his whole life, all while I was supposed to be working.

But what if it was a girl?

Would it be tea parties and Disney movies? I'd have to walk her down the aisle and give her away to a Godly man (when she turned forty, of course, and not a minute sooner). We'd have tough talks and hugs and . . . yep. Pretty soon, I imagined what her life would be like, too. By the time 3 o'clock rolled around and it was time to leave for the appointment, I was pretty confident I'd figured out how to handle either outcome.

Most people had no idea how much I was dwelling on the sex of my first child. "It doesn't matter, as long as it's healthy," I'd tell people when they asked if I was excited to find out. That phrase rolled off my tongue so easily that I didn't even realize what I was saying. Other people said it all the time. It seemed an even-keeled thing to say, and I thought I avoided coming off as a nervous new dad.

I met Tiffany at the doctor's office, and soon we had our answer: we were having a girl. I was thrilled. I was going to be thrilled no matter what, of course, but I was so excited. Who knows? Maybe she'd be interested in learning a jump shot. And suddenly, tea parties sounded amazing.

"Someone wanted a girl," the nurse said as we gathered our things in the reception area. "He hasn't stopped smiling since y'all came out of the room."

Yes, there was a goofy smile on my face, and when I got in my car and turned on the radio, that smile got even bigger. Steven Curtis Chapman's song "Cinderella" was playing, and now I finally understood. A daddy and his princess. That was my future. I detoured on my way home, buying a copy of that CD so I could listen to it on the way to work, running errands, on the way home. I pictured how wonderful it was going to be, a pink-hued sunset of perfection every day.

But in the days before our daughter Payton's birth, things didn't go quite right. There was some trauma leading up to, and during, her birth. We were new parents, so we didn't really grasp that something was wrong at first. We had nothing to compare it to.

Payton couldn't gain weight. She'd throw up nearly everything we fed her. She seemed listless. We tried what seemed like every formula and every recommendation on the planet, but with no success. I was working multiple jobs at the time, and the long nights struggling with this was creating incredible amounts of stress.

In the coming months, we wore a groove in the pavement to and from the hospital as Payton was given the label of "failure to thrive" when they couldn't find what was wrong with her. It felt like we lived our life either at the hospital or the doctor's office as they ran test after test. Test her breathing, test her eyesight, test her blood for genetic disorders. They could find nothing, which was a relief; but watching my little princess get jabbed and prodded was so hard.

Finally, our doctor set us up with an appointment with the chief neurologist at the Dallas Children's Medical Center. As a new parent, it didn't occur to me that that was a sign of something serious: people don't meet the top doctor at one of the biggest children's hospitals in the world if everything is fine. I was just thrilled we were getting such expert testing and consultation, so we went in hoping for the best and thinking we'd finally have our answer on how to fix the problem.

Then, the doctor came back into the room where we waited, carrying a box of tissues.

"There's no easy way to tell you this," he said. "Your daughter only has 10 percent brain function."

My heart seemed to stop, as if the floor gave way and terror had gripped it.

"Barring a miracle," the doctor continued, "she'll never be able to walk, she'll never be able to talk, and if she does, it will be with a very limited vocabulary of about 250 words or less."

I wanted him to stop talking. His voice faded as I was overcome with a wave of grief and sadness that drowned out the horrible reality he was describing.

"She'll never be able to use her hands, or grasp things like a pencil, but"—the doctor tried to inject hope in his voice—"she may be able to use her arms to hug or hold a teddy bear."

> *It's strange how the world can keep turning for everyone else and can stop for you.*

She was legally blind. She wouldn't see detail, though she could see shapes and colors. He went on and on, as best he could, giving us a litany of bad news and crushing the dreams we had for our little princess. He was very sorry to have to tell us this, he said. He made sure we had tissues. He had to be on his way to the next patient. He had tried to be kind, but how can you deliver that news kindly? And then he was gone, and all we heard were his footsteps down the hallway and the screaming silence in the room as we both wept.

It's strange how the world can keep turning for everyone else and can stop for you.

It's in those moments you discover a truth about your relationship with Jesus. You never know it lurks in you, the sense that because of your hard work for the Lord, you deserve something better, you should get to go through life without deep hurt. I had no idea that was in my heart until then, and over time, my prayers turned from sincere hope for healing for my baby girl into complaints and questions rooted in bitterness.

Why me? Why us? I was broken and felt betrayed by God. *God, I work hard for you. I work extra jobs so I can be a youth pastor. I make a difference in people's lives. I don't ask for much. Why would you let this happen to us?*

I began slipping into deep depression, even though my wife was handling the challenges we faced with Payton with incredible grace and strength. In a way, that only made me feel worse. Me, the husband, the father, the pastor, stumbling and complaining and angry with God. What kind of dad feels this way? Didn't I love Payton? Wasn't she a beautiful gift just as she was? Wasn't I supposed to be the strong one in the family?

It's not fair, I thought over and over. *It's not fair to me. To us. To Payton.*

Payton was being cheated; she was going to miss out in this life. Every parent wants the best for their child, and my girl wouldn't even have Cinderella tea parties. She might not even be able to say my name. The weight of disappointment and depression and anger with God was crushing me. It was so heavy, it almost seemed as if it were a tangible pain. It's something I've never experienced since.

Now that I'm on the other side of things, I understand that God loves me and knows me better than I know myself, far more than I can comprehend. And because of that, I know He didn't abandon me, even though the prayers coming from me during that time were awful. I'd be embarrassed to repeat them to you now! God knew we were hurting. He knew the future we'd imagined had just been shattered, and He could handle all the hard questions we were throwing at Him. In fact, God was at work the very day we got Payton's diagnosis, one of those examples of how you can't always see his hands at work until later when you look back.

Ricky and Andrea.

We'd invited our best friends over for dinner the night of the appointment with the specialist, long before we knew what the day would become. We considered canceling because neither of us felt like being around anyone, but I had this sense that we should go ahead. At least it would be a distraction, a moment of normalcy when everything was upside down.

My friend Ricky and Andrea, his wife, have always brought a lot of fun and laughter in our lives. They've helped us at the church, and we've been through a lot together. They came over, and while we were more subdued than usual, the meal went fine.

When the meal was over, we told them what the doctor had told us about Payton, just a few hours earlier. Ricky immediately asked if he could pray for Payton, and he began praying and crying over her for at least five minutes.

I had no idea what he was saying to God. He was praying in Spanish. But I felt an almost tangible peace of God flow into the room and wrap around me. It's that peace that passes all understanding, the peace that has no business being present in the midst of the worst day of your life, but still God puts it there. On the most difficult day of our life, God sent us peace.

But I still had a long way to go.

Bittersweet

Depression is like a choke collar. You have a moment where you feel it loosen, and then it snaps back in a vengeance. It's as if you'll never be free from it, and the good moments make the difficult times all that much harder.

My depression raged on, affecting my wife, my work, and my relationship with God. After talking to Ricky and Andrea about how I was struggling, we all decided to take a vacation to the Alabama seashore. A change of scenery and routine would help, we thought. But even a beautiful rented condo right on the beach couldn't put a dent in the downward spiral.

Perfect location, best friends, and I felt miserable. It became the climax of my depression.

Everywhere I looked, I saw parents with their kids. Dads playing with kids on the beach. Kids burying their dads in the sand. Dads throwing kids into the pool. Dads and their kids building sandcastles.

"Hey, Andy," I could almost hear the enemy say. "That'll never be you."

Finally, after another sleepless night, I got up around 4:30 a.m. and crept out of the condo by myself. It was still dark, at the edge of sunrise where only the barest hint of light hit the horizon and the stars were sparkling above. The sound of the water rolling in and out was background noise to my thoughts. As I walked along the beach, I spotted a couple in front of me doing something very curious.

They'd walk a bit, and then stop and bend down to pick something up. They'd look at it, pause, and then toss whatever it was they had back into the water. Once in a while they kept what they picked up. I walked a bit faster to get closer until I could see what they were doing.

The soft sand was covered with seashells, and they were busy picking them up. They only seemed to keep them if they were whole, and what was broken or imperfect was tossed aside. Once I realized what was happening, I stopped. I let them walk far ahead, down the beach.

This moment is burned into my memory, so much that as I write this, I can fill chills down my back. Because in that very moment, as I looked at the broken shells that the couple had discarded, I heard the Lord say "there's beauty in the broken."

Everything crumbled. Every wall, every fortress of anger and bitterness. The pressure and the burdens all gave way, and everything I'd carried since that day in the doctor's office spewed out of me. I broke down and sobbed.

Let me tell you, it was an ugly cry. And I didn't care.

Through wracking tears, I picked up every broken shell the couple had tossed, placing them in the front of my shirt that I'd pulled out to use as a basket. I must have collected one hundred broken shells that morning, but brokenness—and beauty—was everywhere, stretching down the beach so far I couldn't see the end.

Trudging back to the condo with my shirt full of seashells and my eyes red and watery, I knew something had changed. Tiffany and I had a good cry. She found a glass vase shaped like a shell that we put those broken shells in, something we have on display in our house to this day. Who but God could have used the coquina shells, the cerith shells, the sand dollars—remnants of once-living creatures, broken long before we ever arrived, waiting on the sand for me to see, discarded or ignored by others—to bring healing?

If you visit the Alabama seashore, one of the shells you'll find on that beach is called the bittersweet. It's a common seashell, white and fan-shaped with a corrugated surface usually covered in reddish or brown line patterns. Originating from the saltwater clam family, the bittersweet's shell colors can fade over time as the natural elements wear down the surface. What had been inside died first, and then, over time and the wear of the waves and sand, the shell is smoothed down into soft white and peach colors, rough edges gone, as lovely as a pearl.

There's beauty in the broken.

That was the start of my journey out of depression.

I say it was a journey because it didn't happen all at once. God has a way of leading us through, putting us in the right moments with the right people at the right time. What we think is a coincidence or unconnected is part of how He connects everything, eventually, into a much bigger picture than we could imagine. Nothing is wasted—not a hurt, not a win, not a failure, not a success. All things work together.

God can even use channel surfing.

One evening, still working through my depression, I was flipping through the TV channels and stumbled upon an evangelist. I felt compelled to watch, and the man talked about his new book, *Why Is God So Mad at Me?* He had my attention, and I ordered that book. It ended up being a significant part of what helped me get victory over my battle with depression.

Who was that evangelist? Pat Schatzline.

Years after that night of channel surfing, when my wife and I had won a trip to Greece (which was a miracle in itself), we discovered that the Schatzlines had also won the same trip. Imagine the incredible love of God, the way He weaves our story so perfectly even when we only see a knotted mess. I went from flipping through channels to reading a book to sharing a dinner table with the man whose words had helped me push through.

You can be sure I told him what an impact it had. Ultimately, my wife and I became friends with the Schatzlines, the same wonderful people who later received my texts about the struggles I was having and the

*There's beauty
in the broken.*

admission that I was still broken, and yet still invited me to share our story in South Africa.

Don't you tell me God doesn't know your hurt. Don't you tell me he doesn't care. Don't you try to debate whether he orders our steps. I *know* He does.

When there's an obstacle in front of you, you have two options: quit, or look for the beauty in the broken. God created wins for me, but they wouldn't have come if I'd quit.

Remember the first part of John 10:10, a verse I shared at the start of this chapter? We find out that Satan's sole goal is to kill and destroy. He leaves brokenness in his wake. But then there's the second part of that scripture, the good news that follows the bad. Jesus tells us that He has "come to give life to the fullest."

On the other side of fear and brokenness is life to the fullest. Beauty, amazing accomplishment, crazy dreams you could never have imagined coming true. I know this is true personally, but I assure you that I'm nothing special. If I can see this, if God can do this in me, He will do the same in you. His love for you is just as fierce.

In the coming chapters, I'm going to paint you a real picture of hope, one I lived out brushstroke by brushstroke. It's everything I've learned along the way, but I can only point you to that hope. You hold the key to whatever box or cell you've locked yourself in, the ability to decide to either quit or look for beauty in the broken.

If you're tired of playing it safe, let's journey to the other side of fear.

CHAPTER 2

Beauty in the Broken Prayers

Cabo San Lucas stretches down like a finger along the Pacific Ocean, one of those places where the scenery is almost too beautiful to be possible. Rich blue-green water laps up against soft, sandy shores, with jagged rock formations rooted in the water. In the reddish hills, flecked with bits of desert shrubbery and giant resorts, my wife and I were having an emotional reboot. We'd spent an incredible time connecting with some of the most amazing leaders, and we were enjoying our sunny beach surroundings. It was impossible to imagine anything bad could happen in that setting.

We had one day left in our retreat where we were literally surrounded by hundreds of our business partners and friends. We were sitting out in the sun, trying to soak in as much as we could before we left, having great conversations. That was when Tiffany's phone rang. Just a few seconds into the conversation, I could tell our trip was about to be cut short. I was trying to focus on the conversation with my friends, but I could tell something was up. Something important.

As soon as the phone conversation ended, Tiffany was up and gathering her things.

"We have to get home," she said urgently. "We have to get home, *now*."

After a rush of packing up our room and finding a ride to the airport, we made it back to Dallas by early that evening. Tiffany dropped me off at the hospital where one of our four nurses had taken Payton. She'd been in so much pain, and they couldn't figure out what was causing it.

Payton can't speak. She can only cry to indicate pain, and crying was all she'd been doing, causing her blood pressure to skyrocket. I knew she had to be at the hospital, but we weren't really thrilled about her being there. There was this little pandemic thing happening, you see. The last place we wanted to take her was where she'd be in the thick of it, where her already weak immune system—one so ineffective that she got sick from everything—would be tested.

The doctors worked feverishly, trying to figure out what was happening until late in the evening. They finally figured out Payton needed to have her gallbladder removed, a surgery she couldn't have until the next morning.

"We'll monitor her closely and keep her comfortable," they told us, explaining that the team they'd need to do the surgery on someone with Payton's needs couldn't be there until the morning.

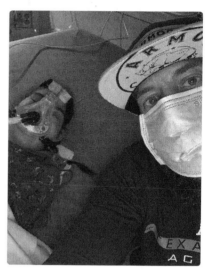

Payton and me in the hospital.

I saw a couch in Payton's room, and I knew where I'd be spending the night. I'm 6'3", and when I laid down on that vinyl hospital couch, my legs ran out of room fast. But I got to be with Payton, and that was a special time. She spends much of her time with the nurses who care for her at home, and this was a chance for me to be with her during a difficult time. I sang and prayed with her, trying to distract her from the pain and the tears. The next morning, they removed her gallbladder, and we could see an immediate difference. She recovered nicely, and soon we had her back home.

I've said a lot of prayers on those tiny hospital couches.

> *I've said a lot of prayers on those tiny hospital couches.*

We do battle there, Payton, the Lord, and I. Just two months earlier, she'd had major spinal surgery. Payton has scoliosis, and for years she had what we called "magic rods," two inserted rods that grew with her spine as she grew. They were adjusted with magnets instead of surgery, but the time had come where we needed to put permanent titanium rods in place. They also fused her vertebrae to help straighten her spine as much as they could to remove the pressure on her lung, helping her breathe better.

Surgeries are always scary, especially with Payton. The spinal surgery had us nervous; meeting the enormous team that would help with the surgery gave us an inkling of how serious this was. And then, of course, all the waivers we had to sign. Waiver after waiver, confusing and intimidating, seemingly endless.

"What's this about permission for a blood transfusion?" I asked the nurse, pointing to one of the documents on the clipboard.

"During this kind of surgery, patients tend to lose a lot of blood. But we'll be monitoring for that," she said.

Another doctor came by just as I was envisioning all the blood. "I'll be in the room watching to make sure the surgeon doesn't get too close to the brain or her nerves along the spine," he said.

Not. Helping.

I gave Payton a kiss as they wheeled her away for surgery. I couldn't go any further with her into the operating room. She had to go there alone. Except, of course, she wasn't alone.

Lee and Jacki, pastors and friends from West Virginia, told me how the Lord had laid Payton on their heart one morning during Sunday worship. Jacki said she saw Payton physically lying in bed, but her spirit was sitting up in the bed playing a game of checkers with Jesus. She could tell they were quite close.

That has meant a lot to me over the years as we've traveled and had to leave Payton at home for her own health. And it meant a lot to me as I watched her being wheeled away for surgery, knowing her friend Jesus would be with her. We wouldn't know how it went until it was over. Eight hours later, we had our answer.

"The surgery went very well," the surgeon told us. Payton's spine had already started fusing in some places, and it had made her job much easier.

A Life Full of Scars

Payton has a lot of scars on her body from these surgeries. My wife has lots of scars, too, running up her arms and legs and around her waist. After she lost weight, she had skin removal surgery. But those are the kinds of scars you can see. God could show us even more scars, the ones in our hearts.

I was there when Kim, Tiffany's sister, was removed from life support and she took her last breath. I was there when her dad, Gary, first learned we were expecting Payton, and he broke down into tears as he told us he had brain cancer and would not be here by the time Payton was born. We have the scars from when we learned of Payton's cerebral palsy and reduced brain function. We have the scars from a miscarriage. We have scars, both big and small, that you pick up along the way in life.

Gary on the day we learned we were expecting Payton and the day he told us he had terminal brain cancer.

These are permanent scars you carry in your heart. But scars are marks of completion, of healing. You were hurt, but now you're whole. They help you become who you are. 2 Corinthians 1:3–4 tells us that God uses those hurts, those things that cause scars, to help us help others. God doesn't wound us, but He never wastes a wound we are given.

I see this at work in Tiffany. She's gone through so much but is at a place where her story inspires thousands. Through her business, she has walked with clients amidst tremendously difficult times—poverty, abuse, family trauma—and because of her scars, she can listen and weep and pray with them. Through her scars, I've watched her grow as a mom and as a Christian in her faith.

Scars are beautiful. They make up who you are. They tell your story. And whether those scars are on the outside or hidden within, they serve as a reminder that we aren't where we used to be, and that we're going somewhere. We were hurt, we healed, we overcame, and we're moving on.

Sometimes, though, we think our scars mean we're weak. We got hurt, and it's still tender. We're still learning to live with the imperfections crisscrossing our body and our heart.

I prayed for Payton for years after her diagnosis. It became almost second nature. There was still pain, and because of that, there was still hope. But Payton wasn't healed, and then the question became a difficult one, something people who have faced hurt and pain often come to: Is it because my faith is too weak?

"God, heal it up so there's no scar," we essentially pray. "This hurts, and I don't want this."

I struggled with that, I'll be honest. Did I have weak faith? Were my prayers broken? Was God ignoring me?

During this time in my life, I was at a youth pastor's conference, and I struggled to focus on the training and activity. It was so hard to be there, outwardly in the ministry, inwardly carrying the weight of Payton and my unanswered prayers on my shoulders. My scars were open wounds.

One evening, as we all gathered for worship and the dimmed lights and music filled the auditorium, I felt the Lord speak to me.

"Dude, you're holding onto this burden too tightly," He said (he doesn't seem to speak to me in KJV). The music around me kept going, but I was attuned to what was happening. "You weren't meant to carry that kind of weight. Let me help you. My burden is easy and light."

"I've been holding on so tight, like I'm white knuckling a roller coaster," I later told my brother when we met for dinner afterward.

You know what happens when you get off of a roller coaster after you've been gripping it with all your strength?

Your hands hurt. And you're still scared because you were scared when you were gripping and your hands are still feeling the grip.

God did not answer my prayer for Payton the way I wanted Him to.

God did not answer our prayers for Tiffany's sister, Kim.

God did not answer our prayers for Tiffany's dad, Gary.

But Kim's death did bring Gary back to Christ, and he's now in Heaven, living in eternity. That's eternal healing, and I don't mean that as a fall-back, feel-good response when it seems God doesn't answer our prayers.

Maybe my prayers didn't go unanswered in the midst of all of these many broken situations. In Isaiah 55:8–9, God makes it clear that He is not like us. "My thoughts aren't your thoughts," He gently reminds us. "My ways aren't your ways."

He knows our pain, He hears our prayers, and He answers in pure love. But His ways are not our ways.

Getting Full Immunity

When Tiffany and I were first married, we liked to watch the TV show *The Biggest Loser*. We found it inspiring because we were both struggling with our weight at that time. (Of course, we'd watch people exercising and doing the work while sitting on the couch eating.) One of the interesting things on that show is something called immunity. If a contestant won an immunity card through an obstacle or challenge, they could not lose weight and would still get to stay on the show at least one more week.

Through the years, I've wondered what Payton would have been like if things had been different. Payton isn't a baby anymore; she's thirteen. I've watched her cousins, all born within six months of each other, grow up into wonderful, beautiful girls. When I see them or other kids around Payton's age playing sports or having fun with family, it hurts.

But then I realize Payton has her very own immunity card. She will never lose her innocence. She only has a future in eternity with her friend Jesus, a future where she's free from the prison of her broken body. She will be able to see and speak and sing and dance, grab a paintbrush and create beautiful art. She'll only see her nurses if she wants to hang out with them and chill for a while. I bet Payton's first word will be "Jesus"! How could it get any better than that?

What more could a parent ask for than for their child to make it to Heaven for eternity? Life on this earth, in the here and now, is fragile. It's just a drop in the bucket compared to what's coming. All our gains and accomplishments are meaningless compared to our eternal reward in Heaven.

Heaven is so costly for being a free gift. Romans 6:23 tells us that "the wages of sin is death, but the gift of God is eternal life in Christ Jesus our Lord."

Think about that! Our bill for sin is death. *Forever.* Eternal death is where we're all headed. That's heavy stuff. Romans also reminds us that we've all sinned, that we've all fallen short of the glory of God.

Payton's friend Jesus has some scars of His own to prove that. Sometimes, I wonder if they compare scars during their checker games.

"Look, Payton," He might say. "These scars on my hands and feet are for you. I've got some pretty gnarly scars on my ribs and back, too. I'm covered in them. All for you."

Jesus picked up that tab for *all* our sins.

He laid down his own life to pay our bill in full. We hear the story so much that it becomes commonplace, that it loses its shine. But I want you to think about what Jesus did as if it's the first time you're hearing it.

And if it is the first time you heard it?

Good news: Jesus didn't stay dead! He not only died, but He rose from the dead, and now, if anyone calls on His name and believes He is the Son of God, they'll also live for eternity in Heaven.

It's the ABCs of salvation: Admit you're not perfect, that you've sinned. Believe that Jesus is the Son of God and that He came to die for your sins. Confess that Jesus is Lord, because when He rose from the grave, He provided victory over eternal death for us.

It seems too simple, but that's it. You don't have to pray eloquently; God loves simple, heartfelt prayers that are earnest and come from a sincere heart. And if you prayed and asked Jesus to save you, find a good

" What more could a parent ask for than for their child to make it to Heaven for eternity? "

church home and a pastor or a trusted friend who can help you start walking it out in this life.

Guess what happens in Heaven when anyone prays that prayer?

A huge party. Yes, a *huge* party, a massive celebration over your decision.

It's the single most important decision you ever make in your life, the most important prayer you'll ever pray. And if you're struggling with the fact that you've said a lot of broken prayers over the years, know that God—your creator—has heard, and that He knows best. Trust the One you're praying to, that He holds the treasure of a broken heart and a broken spirit and responds in the best way.

When I let go of Payton in the hospital and left her in the hands of a doctor that day, it was much easier knowing I was also leaving her in the hands of her good friend Jesus, trusting His ways for her life.

You can do the same with your prayers. Let Jesus's beautiful, scarred hands hold them.

CHAPTER 3

The Comeback

In 1993, it seemed like a bad time to be a Buffalo Bills fan. The Houston Oilers had soundly beat them earlier in the season, and it was clear that history was repeating itself in the playoffs. I was sprawled across the couch, watching the rather sad NFL playoff game between the two teams when my brother Tim walked into the room.

Pausing for a moment, he looked at the third quarter score. 35-3, Oilers all the way.

"This one's over," he said, then walked out.

I call that the Tim Howard Jinx (THJ for short). He has a dubious gift, though it seemed at that moment he couldn't be wrong. The Bills were so far down, and relying on a backup quarterback on top of it, that I had to agree with Tim. Even the fans in Buffalo had all but emptied out of the stadium, the television cameras panning across ever-emptying seats with sports announcers signaling the end for the Bills.

But then, in the final quarter, the Bills rallied. In ten plays they drove fifty yards, scoring a touchdown, and then another touchdown off a wayward kick. Interceptions and a solid mix of passing and running brought the teams' scores within four points of each other in just under seven minutes.

I was off the couch at that point.

The game went to overtime, with the Oilers struggling to push back against the energized Bills team. A thirty-two-yard field goal sealed the deal, and the Bills won. They made it to the Super Bowl.

In sports history, that game became known as the Comeback.

There's something amazing when you watch a comeback happening, when the little guy pulls ahead, the loser becomes the winner, the weak are suddenly strong. I remember something similar in 2016 when my team, the Texas A&M Aggies, were playing the Northern Iowa Panthers (UNI). With only thirty-five seconds left in the game, my Aggies were down by twelve. It was pure agony.

Tiffany saw me slumped over on the chair.

"You have a problem," she said

Yeah, I do, it's a twelve-point problem.

She probably meant that maybe I'm a little too emotionally attached to my teams, and I guess she's right. It was clear my Aggies were going to lose, and yet I still couldn't turn off the TV. Instead, I sat in my chair, hunched down with my arms crossed, sulking, waiting for the end. I later read that with that much of a lead and only thirty-five seconds left, UNI had a 99.99 percent chance of winning, because what better use for math is there than sports statistics? You couldn't blame me for feeling a bit sour at that moment.

But then my Aggies rallied. They began pressing and quickly forced four turnovers. UNI didn't get past the half court line. Somehow, after a 14-2 run during regulation time, they forced the game into overtime and pulled off the win. If Tiffany thought I had a problem before, the whooping and hollering that came from the living room cemented it in her mind.

The exhilaration a sports fan feels at a comeback is nothing compared to seeing a comeback in someone's life.

He Gives and Takes Away

When Tiffany and I finally decided to have more children, we were terrified.

There was no shortage of doctors telling us not to, since they couldn't determine if Payton's condition was genetic or not. They warned us of the risks: if it was a genetic disorder, our future children could have the same problem.

We prayed. A lot. We understood the risk. We lived it every day. Tiffany even told me that, after seeing the toll Payton's illness took on me, she wondered if I'd hold up if it happened to another child.

"I feel at peace about it now," I told her, and I was being honest. "I'm ready."

One morning, I went in to check on Payton, and Tiffany was standing there. She had dressed Payton in a shirt that said "Big Sister." Now, admittedly, I didn't catch it at first. I didn't catch it at second either.

"I think she's trying to tell you something, Daddy," Tiffany said gently, nudging me to really take in the scene.

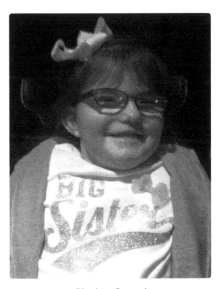

Big sister Payton!

Wow! I got lost in the moment, but it felt like hours because so many emotions flooded over me. Was this really happening? Were we ready? Because of Payton, we were already connected with a great doctor in Dallas, one who handled high-risk pregnancies. The previous pregnancy with Payton qualified us to work with him, and so we contacted him right away.

Our first appointment rolled around, and we were excited. Tiffany was on the exam table, and the doctor was doing a sonogram. He was very quiet, working intently for a long time, until he abruptly wiped the gel off of Tiffany's stomach.

"Let's sit tight," he said. "I want to call a friend of mine here in the hospital who's a specialist. He has some equipment in his office that could help check something out."

We were told to wait. It was excruciating.

Not again. Lord, please. No, I'm sorry, Lord, it's in Your hands. But please, Lord.

Was it happening all over? Minutes felt like hours, and while we were both quiet, we gripped each other's hands in the waiting room, praying.

Soon, we were ushered into the specialist's office, and it didn't take him long to check Tiffany.

"I'm so sorry to tell you this, but your baby doesn't have a heartbeat," he said. "You'll have to have a D and C. The sooner the better, to protect Tiffany."

No.

I'd told the world we were having a baby. I put it out on social media. I told everyone I met. I was so excited, and I didn't know about waiting until after the first trimester. And now, to the degree that I had spread the news and happiness, we'd have to reap the sympathetic and sometimes awkward comments from people.

"We heard you expecting! How far along?" people would ask.

"We lost the baby."

Then an awkward pause, followed by stumbling sympathies. This happened over and over, and it was like ripping open a wound every time. I couldn't blame people; they weren't trying to hurt us.

The first Sunday back in church after we'd lost the baby, the worship team led a song that had lyrics that seemed directed right at us. "You give and take away. You give and take away," the team sang. "My heart will choose to say, blessed be your name."

Tiffany heard it. She received it as a direct message from God that everything was going to be OK. She was so strong, and she still is. But I was struggling.

The Strong of Heart

Comebacks are hard. We cheer when we see them; we don't get as excited to cheer on things that seem easy.

> *Comebacks are not for the faint of heart.*

Comebacks are not for the faint of heart. They force you to gather up all your hope and faith and go all in, all over again. It's why most people quit before they get a chance to have a comeback.

Kirk Gibson, of the Los Angeles Dodgers, was hurting. He had injured both of his legs and wasn't even in the Dodgers' lineup that first game of the 1988 World Series. Yet when the Dodgers were down in the bottom of the ninth, with two outs, he was called up to pinch hit. The win or the loss rested on injured Gibson. As he stiffly made his way to the plate, the crowd stood to its feet, roaring, while the announcers were surprised to see him walk onto the field. This was it.

Dennis Eckersley, the tough Oakland A's closer, got Gibson buried under strikes and fouls until there was no more leeway left. It didn't look good for the Dodgers, and Gibson's legs seemed stiffer with every swing of the bat. Gibson dug his feet deep into the dirt, trying to find a position of strength despite his injury.

Eckersley eyeballed Gibson, maybe figuring he was down for the count, and threw a slider. But relying on his upper body strength and not his injured legs, Gibson knocked that ball high into right field—a home run. I remember watching the crowd go wild, knowing they'd just won the game, as Gibson limped around the bases to home plate and into a wall of ecstatic teammates who'd rushed the field the moment the ball was gone. Gibson had a bum knee and a rotten hamstring, but a strong heart.

It was remarkable, but what was more remarkable was that just like the Buffalo Bills game, many fans had left the stadium. They decided they'd rather beat the traffic than watch their team get beat, and they ended up missing out on a great story to tell their kids and grandkids. Maybe they'd have to be satisfied telling them how they heard it on the radio while sitting in the Chavez Ravine parking lot next to Dodger Stadium. Maybe they'd hang their head and admit that they were in one of those cars who slammed on their brakes as the announcer blurted out the home run, the red brake lights splashing across the top of the screen as the camera followed Gibson around the field.

There's nothing as good as a comeback, and it's even better when you're there, seeing it happen before your eyes.

Our friends Austin and Monique know about comebacks.

Austin had a good childhood. It'd be safe to say it was traditional. He was raised in the suburbs with two caring parents and an older sister. Education and sports were important in the home, and church on Sunday was always a must. He'll be the first to say his parents and the adults in his life taught him good morals and values, about how to work hard and believe in the abilities God had given him. Yet things were still tough for him.

"I always felt anxious around other kids," Austin admitted to me once. "It was like I didn't fit in, even though I had friends."

What resulted was a life of drugs and alcohol.

"Drug dealing and turning my back on God went against everything I'd been taught my entire life," he told me. "So, I became a liar. I hid stuff. I acted like everything was OK so no one would find out what I was doing."

But you can't hide alcoholism and drug use forever.

For eighteen months, Austin lived in a rundown apartment with his dog. He had tried to get clean, but he relapsed and lost his job. His only social interaction was with his drug dealer, and he'd only reach out to his family to get money.

"An average day would be waking up shaking from withdrawal and then scrounging up some money to get alcohol," he said. "I'd go home and drink until I passed out. I hated myself. I thought about suicide a lot. I only knew how to pray foxhole prayers, asking God to keep me from overdosing or getting arrested or dying."

Monique grew up in New York City with a single mom and her aunts for the first five years of her life. They were very close, and she knew she was loved. Her biological father had remarried but was still part of her life until one day she went to visit him and discovered he was gone. They had moved to Florida and hadn't told her.

"I felt abandoned," she said. "For a long time, I thought he left because of me."

Her mother also remarried, and soon, she saw her stepdad as her dad and took his last name. But in hindsight, she can see that her upbringing wasn't very normal at all. It was chaos, in fact.

"My grandfather was a mobster, and that lifestyle spilled into all of our lives," she told me. "I learned to hustle at a very young age."

By age sixteen, Monique was into drugs and alcohol, but she also took diet pills that contained Ephedra.

"I was completely bulimic," she said, "but I hid it well. I was a chameleon and could fit into any friend group, but I was dying inside."

One night, after partying to numb the pain, she attempted suicide. She wrote a letter and downed a bottle of pills. She ended up in the ICU but survived. Then, at age seventeen, she found out she was pregnant. She'd always wanted to be a mom, but she wasn't allowed to keep the baby and was forced to have an abortion.

"The one thing I wanted, I wasn't allowed to keep," she said.

Her drug abuse and partying increased, and Monique hit rock bottom at age twenty-five after a terrible drug and alcohol binge. She finally cried out to God for help; and just ten minutes later, an aunt from Florida called, bought her a plane ticket, and set her up in a rehab center.

Monique and Austin eventually met each other, got married, and soon had children. They still struggled with things from their past but worked hard to move forward together.

Two broken lives, two broken strands of thread whose stories God wove together. If you listened to Austin and Monique tell you their story, you'd never believe it. They're a beautiful family with four amazing kids, and they've created a wonderful partnership both in marriage and in their own coaching business that has absolutely exploded! Health is an important part of their lives, and they've now helped thousands of others on the same path.

Austin and Monique.

How do you go from passing out on the floor of a cockroach-infested apartment, or waking up from a binge, to leading others on a path toward health and wholeness? How do you turn it around like that?

Comebacks take a strong heart, and they often require a crossroads.

Standing At the Crossroads

The story of my nephew Zak is another moving comeback story.

His childhood was full of love from his parents and a strong upbringing. All the things you hope to provide for your children, his parents provided. But by doing that, Zak was sheltered, and he didn't understand how some things worked in the world. He didn't see the ugly until he was older. That's not a bad thing, but it has a different impact on people.

Zak had been heavily involved in church, where his dad was a pastor; but after his first year at a Christian university, something changed. He didn't go back to school, and instead he moved into an apartment with friends, where he picked up a lifestyle of drugs, alcohol, and partying.

You hear stories like this all the time: people telling you how they got involved in drugs and alcohol. And while you agree it's terrible, it doesn't quite have the same impact as it does for those entangled in the story. This was *my* nephew. *My* people. It tore me up to hear it.

Zak asked to move home, he agreed to follow the rules, and that seemed like a good ending to the story. It seemed like he had gone through a rough patch but came to a crossroads and had finally chosen the right path.

But that's not what happened.

Through a convoluted set of bad choices, bad friends, lying, and continued drug use, Zak unintentionally found himself embroiled in a murder.

One night Zak was partying with some people he didn't know well. One of the guys asked Zak to accompany him to collect some money that a young man owed him. The plan was for Zak and his brand-new acquaintance to then take that money and score more drugs to keep the party going.

When the pair showed up to meet the young man, Zak's mutual partyer told him, "Just wait here, I'll just be a minute. I'll shout if I need you."

Zak waited. That was when he heard the gunshots. He was terrified, under the influence, and made the very poor decision to flee the scene. Unbeknownst to Zak, his acquaintance had a gun and killed the young man in cold blood. In seconds the situation went from drug deal to murder. And instead of telling his family what happened or going to the authorities, because he was so terrified of what would happen to his family or himself, he sat on it and hoped no one would find out. But God loved Zak too much to let that fester in his life. The police eventually arrested Zak as an accomplice, and he was sentenced to eighteen years in prison.

It was a tragedy all around. Zak was in the wrong place at the wrong time and made an awful decision. And that poor young man senselessly lost his life for a few dollars to a drug dealer.

Yes, my nephew is in prison now. Ironically, it is the place where he has finally found freedom.

On Zak's first day in jail, he rededicated his life to the Lord. I'm not going to say things are easy now, or that it was anything but painful for the whole family; but just like with Austin and Monique, God has made the broken so beautiful.

God took that mess of drugs and death and deceit and turned my nephew Zak into a missionary for the Lord, right there in prison. He's led so many inmates to Jesus through Bible studies and conversations. And when they want to be baptized, two inmates lower the new Christ-follower backward

The last picture Zak and I took before he was arrested a few months later.

so Zak can "baptize" him by pouring water from a cup on their head.[3]

He still has to own his mistakes—but he has become a remarkable man following hard after God. I can't tell you how proud I am of him.

When we see our lives through worldly eyes, we think we only get one chance, one opportunity to get it right, one crossroads to choose the right path. If you fail, if you're not perfect, or if you're broken, it's too late. You're a throwaway human being. You're irredeemable.

But God *loves* comebacks.

We can stand at the crossroads and try to make our own way, or we can stand before the Cross and trust the only Way. God is the Comeback King.

---

3   John W. Kennedy, *"A Prisoner for Christ,"* Assemblies of God (USA), *September 28, 2018, https://news.ag.org/en/News/A-Prisoner-for-Christ.*

God is the Comeback King.

You Need Your Best Players

Losing is not my favorite thing to do (unless we're talking about losing weight). I just hate losing. I'll admit that the mistakes I regret the most in my life aren't actually the things that caused me to lose. It was how I reacted as a sore loser.

By day, pretty mild dude. By night, raging sore loser. That's me.

Don't even talk to me about church softball. I remember one game where a guy on third base started talking smack to me, and pretty soon, we were up in each other's faces saying every awful thing. Somewhere a rooster crowed three times. Actually it was just my dad, the third base coach, eyeballing me with a look that let me know he had heard all the words I'd said, and none of them were acceptable.

That's nothing compared to the church Turkey Bowl that we do every Thanksgiving. We get the "old" guys to take on the young guys, and we produce a heated rivalry that far exceeds the Cowboys vs. Eagles, the Lakers vs. Celtics, and A&M vs. Whiney Orange (sorry, still working on that!).

One year the young guys started their trash talking early. Easy to laugh off until you get on the field, and the halos are stripped away. Pretty soon the miracle of the playing field took over, and the old guys were smoking the young guys. It wasn't long before the joking trash talking turned into this-is-the-Super-Bowl-and-millions-are-on-the-line talking.

"What's going on here?!" one of the deacons finally said. "This is ridiculous. Do you think this is Christlike?"

As we left after the game was over, Tiffany pulled me aside.

"You know you're the youth pastor, right?" she said. Ouch. It was the last Turkey Bowl I ever played in.

I worked hard in the following years to keep my competitive spirit in check. It was destroying me. I would tell myself before anything that could be remotely construed as a competition (sports, hot dog eating contests, getting out of the parking lot) that it didn't matter if I lost. The important thing was holding onto my friends for later in life.

My brother must have known I was slowly dying inside with this new way of living.

"Why not use your competitive spirit for good?" he finally asked me.

Uh, I'm listening!

"Try competing against yourself to make changes," he explained.

Turns out that was a smart suggestion. Self-competition has propelled me to weight loss and a healthy lifestyle. Plus, it's prodded me to write this book.

With my competitiveness directed in a positive direction, things are definitely better. But I still have one major problem with losing, and that's when we lose without our best players in action.

When you have everyone in the game, playing their best, and you still lose, so be it. The other team was better. But when your best players are absent . . . who knows what would have happened?

Some of you are tired of losing and think that you can never win, that you can't have a comeback. The problem is that you're trying to play the game without your team. Some of our best players in life aren't even playing the game. They're sitting in the dark, not using their gifts. They've been hurt and decided they should sit out. The sidelines look safer.

Monique, Austin, and Zak are amazing players, some of the best I know. I asked them what they'd say to someone in need of a comeback.

Monique's answer? Get on your knees, surrender to God, and stop trying to do it on your own. Ask for help. Find your team, your community.

Austin told me we all need to make a simple commitment to move forward, relying on God for strength.

Zak said we needed to be honest about who we are with the people around us, our personal community, and with God.

Three months after we lost our second child, we found out Tiffany was pregnant again. Our doctor had been encouraging, even though I'd come to accept we wouldn't have any more children.

That Sunday, before going into our first appointment, the worship team sang the same song again. At the office, the doctor was quiet during the sonogram again, and then asked us to see the specialist again. We went upstairs and waited again.

Please not again.

"Ah, I see what he was wondering about," the specialist said, looking at the screen. "Congratulations! You're having twins!"

What a comeback!

But you can't have a comeback if you quit.

Remember, there's Kirk Gibson, injured and stiff and on the sidelines, hobbling out to bat, sending a baseball into sports history with his team all around him. There's Monique, Austin, and Zak, far from rock bottom, helping turn broken lives into beauty. There's my wife and me, multiple children in tow.

And then there's you: are you ready for a comeback?

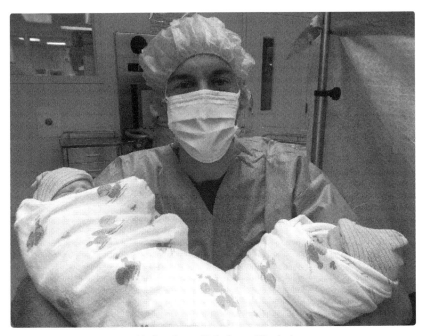

My first photo with Parker and Presley!

CHAPTER 4

Speaking Life or Death

Perched on the southwest tip of the African continent, Cape Town, South Africa looks impossibly situated when you see it from the air. Several mountains that jut out above the city pierce it, cutting it in half. The ocean water is deep blue, and there's an almost donut-looking stadium near the shore. Behind Table Mountain National Park, the rest of the city sprawls out to the north and east. It was about as far away from Texas as you could get.

Pat Schatzline had asked me to come and speak, and so I flew to Cape Town to share Payton's story, our story, in front of thousands of people.

I've prayed many prayers over Payton, but there is one particular prayer that I can now say relates to South Africa. Most of my prayers for Payton would start by praying for her healing, but I'd end with ". . . and Lord, let her story reach millions."

I never understood the power of words or even how that kind of request could ever become a reality. In my limited mind, I thought her story might be how the Lord would heal her someday, a miraculous moment where He'd raise her out of the wheelchair and she'd be able to walk and talk, and the whole thing would go viral. That was how I envisioned it.

In the weeks before I went to South Africa, I'd been listening to the song "Raise a Hallelujah." It's a song about praising God even in the midst of the struggles and trials of life, and the victory that brings. When you're in the worst place, it's the best thing to do. It helped having worship in the background as I prepared for the trip because I needed to partner with God and connect with what He had for me and His people.

I won't kid you, I was scared. I didn't feel qualified to be in South Africa speaking in front of all those people. I'd never spoken in front of that many people in my life, and I didn't have that miraculous story of healing to tell, the one I'd envisioned. People wanted to hear that kind of amazing thing, didn't they? I was almost paralyzed with anxiety over it. I was so focused on my feelings about what I was asked to do that I didn't realize I'd made the whole thing about myself.

What will *I* say? How could *I* help those people? Was *I* ready for this? Could God use *me*?

Only five months earlier, I'd had my texting conversation with Pat about how his sermon had blessed me; and now here I was, asked by Pat to speak in front of thousands and thousands. I was almost held captive by my own thoughts and words, and it took my good buddy JM to give me a bit of a knock about, mentally.

"This isn't about you!" he reminded me. "God's going to use you once you get that in your heart. Don't make it about you. Be free to be used by God instead."

That helped. Sort of.

It's hard to shed the nervousness and energy that comes from facing thousands upon thousands of people listening to the words coming out of your mouth. Tiffany wasn't there with me, and I wasn't used to speaking alone. I called her the night before, and she encouraged me, reminding me again, like my friend, about why I was there.

There were several churches in the Cape Town area where we'd be ministering during the week I was there, and Pat and I split up to reach more churches on that first Sunday morning. My driver picked me up and took me to my first church, a 30-minute trip.

You know what I discovered about long drives? You have more time to get nervous. By the time we pulled into the parking lot, I was nearly choking on fear, and it felt like my important internal organs had rearranged themselves, with my heart in my mouth. In front of me was the church, a building that looked like a metal warehouse with thin walls that did little to mute the sounds from inside. What was said inside could easily be heard outside, too.

Oh, great. The whole world is going to be listening, not just the people inside.

But then I stopped listening to the noise in my head and heard the noise coming from the church. I could hear the praises of God's people, and wouldn't you know it, they were singing "Raise a Hallelujah."

My song. A song that had become like oxygen to me. I'd listened to it almost on constant repeat leading up to this trip. The girls and I would listen on the way to school, on the way home, and everywhere in between.

As the words and music washed over me, I felt at home. When the church got to the chorus, I heard a roar go up as the loud crowd began to cheer, passionately praising Jesus.

My fear was gone. And not only that, but I was seriously exhilarated.

From fearful to powerful.
Only God does that.

I got out of the car and was meeting throngs of people before I even made it inside. Ushers were asking how they could help, and I was meeting pastors from the church campus. I was dying to get inside, like a raging bull waiting for the gate to fly open. Maybe it was the double shot of espresso I'd had, but I think it was the song, the worship, and the confirmation that God had beautifully woven it all together and was in control. From fearful to powerful. Only God does that.

As I walked over the threshold of the doorway, God reminded me of all the prayers I'd sent forward to Him, about how He would use Payton's story to reach millions.

Is this it, God? Is it really happening? Wow, You are so good!

Speaking in South Africa and being used by the Lord thousands of miles from home.

Speaking Life or Death

The power of mindset is no small thing. We're pretty careful not to wander into traffic or off the cliff; but we let our minds wander all over the place, not understanding that where our mind goes, we go. In His Word, God is clear that we have to be careful what we do with our mind, what we put into it, and that we need to control it. Romans 12:2 talks about the importance of renewing your mind instead of falling into the pattern of the world. Philippians 4:8 reminds us to be careful what we let our minds consume.

Our mind determines our attitude, and each day we set the agenda for how that day will go by how our attitude is. Every morning, I start the day off with the same routine of spending time with God before I hit the grind. I ask Him to partner with me and to put people in my path that I can serve.

Proverbs 18:21 tells us that the tongue has the power of life and death, and I want to speak life.

Seriously, hanging around with negative people makes my head hurt. I remember one of my dad's sermons where he said the phrase, "I think myself happy," While I don't remember much else about that sermon, I do hold onto that.

Have you ever noticed how easy it is to get knocked off track? Your day is all sunshine and roses until you spill your coffee, and then the Debbie Downer background music plays. You immediately decide it's just going to be one of those days. You walk out the door expecting the worst, defeated even before you got started. And now, since you're completely tuned into the negative, that's all you'll be able to see in the day. Everything that's wrong, annoying, or imperfect, you'll notice. All the good things will fly right by you.

But you can flip that on its head; if you go out the door with confidence and speak life over yourself, controlling your thoughts and choosing to take a different view of all that is going on around you, your day is totally different. Instead of mourning a spilled cup of coffee, you think, "hey, I bet the next cup will taste even better."

It's the difference between dreading what's next and being excited for what's next. In the first scenario you speak death, while in the second you speak life. It seems like a small thing, but it changes the outcome of your day. The outcome of your day changes the outcome of the week, of the month, of the year, and of your life.

We should walk around with confidence, not in ourselves (which is when we become arrogant and cocky), but in what God is doing in us. I recently counseled a young man who walked into our appointment beat-up but left upbeat. All I did was listen to him voice his struggles, and then I spoke life into him. Your words are powerful.

I need to take my own advice because while I've made some big strides in that area, I don't always believe in myself. In that way, I doubt what God is doing. But partnering with God on a daily basis has been the game changer for me.

Confidence is one of my biggest struggles. I grew up the youngest of five boys in a great family with wonderful parents. We were very close-knit, and even though we don't live near each other now, we still have that deep connection.

My parents were like the king and queen of the small town where we grew up; they loved the community, and it loved them back. Dad would visit nearly every hospital from Tyler to Dallas and spend hours talking to people on the phone telling them how much he missed seeing them on Sunday. He really loved to serve the community; and that meant wherever we went, people knew who we were.

My brothers were talented athletes and musicians, some going into the ministry. But as the youngest, I felt overlooked; this was because the enemy was feeding me a lie.

"Look at your brothers. Look at your parents. How can you live up to that?" he'd prod me.

I was in a family that loved me, but I was floundering because I didn't know if I could live up to their high levels of success. Even my cousins were amazing people, and I was left feeling inadequate. I didn't know if I was enough. But God didn't put those expectations on me; the enemy did. God always makes us enough, never basing His love for us on whether or not we perform correctly.

One year, my uncle, aunt, and cousins came to hold revival services at a church in Terrell, Texas. Tiffany and I weren't married yet, but we went to the service that night. God had given my uncle a special gift; he was so in tune with God that he could speak into the lives of people and say the very thing they needed to hear from God. I'd seen it happen before and was always amazed. I remember the time he walked up to a waitress in a restaurant and spoke life into her. She was there to serve us, but instead, she was being served; and I watched tears roll down her cheeks as she thanked him.

But it was always something I watched him do for others until that night at the revival service. He called Tiffany and I to the front, and I was nervous about what was going to happen. Yet I trusted my uncle.

He said, "Andy, the Lord sees you, and you are coming out of your brothers' shadows to be used greatly."

I have no idea what happened after that because it was a blur. I was so overwhelmed with peace; and while I tried to pay attention and remember what else was said, it didn't matter. I'd heard what I needed to hear: the literal words I needed spoken out loud to me to counteract the internal lies the enemy had been filling me with for so long.

Just after Tiffany and I were married, my uncle died. The hurt was real, but I took his words with me for a while. I didn't just sit on those words, of course. I kept looking around every corner to see how God could use me to fulfill them. God doesn't just hand you something ready to go right out of the box. He blesses your efforts as you work where He is working. So, I worked hard. I tried a lot of things to fulfill those words, but I just wasn't seeing it and doubts creeped in. The enemy was happy to suggest that maybe I didn't hear him right, or maybe God had changed His mind. Before long, we'd had Payton and the twins, and life was moving fast. I gradually forgot about that night at the revival.

Other thoughts and words had slipped in.

It's All My Fault

It's funny how God often chooses our busiest seasons of life to do major work in us. Does He not know we're busy? (Of course He does; that's exactly why He does it!) It was during that busy season of life that God decided to get to work in me. In fact, He'd already set the ball in motion a few years earlier.

After we'd gotten Payton's diagnosis, our pastor told us that God had told him we should step down for a season, that the decision was too big for us to make right now, and God needed to make it for us. And he was right. We needed to focus on our family and Payton's needs, and the next few years were going to be all new territory.

But I had no idea what to do with myself being out of ministry. So, I decided to go back to college. There I was, at the community college, the older-than-average guy among the youth. One of my classes was Intro to Psychology, which, initially, I was less than thrilled about. I'd always found therapists a little creepy up to that point (I apologize!). I pictured people laying on couches in front of someone with a notepad, spilling their guts. No thanks.

However, the instructor of that class really made an impression on me and helped me to see that my depression was real. She helped me see that getting help wasn't weak and that I always ought to hang out with people who were trying to better themselves. Because of that positive classroom experience and the never-ending rollercoaster of depression I continued to struggle with, I finally told Tiffany that I needed to find some help. She supported me because she knew what was going on inside and how my self-inflicted words were destroying me.

"You'd never let anyone talk to your wife or kids the way you talk to yourself," she told me.

I found a therapist who was a Christian, and she'd start each session with prayer. She'd use Scripture to support the things she told me during our sessions, speaking true life into me. In the coming months, she helped me unpack all the hurts I'd been carrying in my heart without once making me feel like I was crazy.

But I had a secret.

No one really knew the full story of what happened to Payton. For years, doctors would speculate that it was genetic or have some other theory. But they didn't know what had actually happened.

Tiffany was in labor with Payton for fifty-four hours. Yes, fifty-four hours. I know because I know the 5-1-1 rule, where the labor contractions come every five minutes, lasting one minute each, for at least an hour. She was in labor for fifty-four hours. I'm obsessive about numbers, and believe me, I was tracking this.

We were first-time parents, but I knew something was wrong. Over that fifty-four-hour block of time, we came back to the hospital three different times, trying to get them to admit Tiffany. The doctor would just laugh and send us home.

"Y'all are just so excited, but trust me, you'll know when you're in labor," she'd say.

But I knew Tiffany was in labor. Each time we came in, they had a hard time finding Payton's pulse but would dismiss it as if she was just sleeping. Or they'd tell Tiffany to drink some apple juice or eat a cracker. Then there'd be a little spike in the pulse, and they'd send us home.

By the third trip, Tiffany was dilated to six. But even then, the nurses at the front desk were calm and joking around with us, admiring Tiffany's baby bag and taking photos with it. I understood they saw nervous parents every day, but this was serious to us. Tiffany had been in incredible pain for two full days.

Finally, they got us a room and called our doctor. She said she'd be in later, that it would probably be a while. Tiffany finally got an epidural. But it was given so late—and everything started to move much faster than they'd thought it would—that the doctor didn't make it in time. The nurse there only had time to get one glove on before she delivered our baby girl. The umbilical cord was around Payton's neck, depriving her of oxygen.

This was our first child. We didn't know what was and wasn't normal. They whisked Payton away immediately, and there was tension in the room. They were working to save Payton's life, but they didn't tell us this at the time.

Eventually, they brought her back to us to hold her, and we didn't realize anything was wrong. She was tightly bunched up, her arms and legs in a fetal position, a position that she didn't relax for weeks. They told us that they think it was because she was in the birth canal for so long.

Tiffany and baby Payton.

For fifty-four hours that was happening to Payton.

We didn't sue the hospital. It didn't even cross our minds, and frankly, it wouldn't have made me feel any better. It just felt like we were overlooked and unnoticed, not taken seriously.

My therapist dug into this, and I finally broke.

"It's my fault!" I said. "It's my fault that Payton is the way she is."

I explained how I'd been monitoring Tiffany, how I knew the 5-1-1 rule, how I knew she was in labor; but I'd trusted the doctor instead.

"I wish I would have stood up to her," I said, starting to sob. I hated my obedient, go-along-to-get-along personality. Because I wouldn't confront that doctor and demand something be done about my daughter, she was sentenced to live the rest of her life with all her challenges.

At this point, I was bawling and flinging snot all over. My therapist handed me a tissue. Several, in fact.

"Oh, Andy, you've carried this way too long," she said kindly. "You've literally held yourself hostage. It's as if you had a gun held to your head because you believe this great weight is your fault. It's not your fault. You're not the doctor. You did everything you could."

It was as if God was using her words to unlock the heavy clamp around my chest, removing the shackle that had bound me for so long.

It felt like breathing for the first time after holding my breath for years. She helped me change my mindset and how I saw what had happened. By speaking life into me, she made it possible for me to move forward, no longer a hostage to myself.

I couldn't get to that freedom without being terrifyingly honest and being willing to dig down deep into the darkest, heaviest, most fearful secret I'd harbored, a deadly treasure that I'd allowed to define my life for so long.

So now, I have to ask: What about you?

What you've just read, only a few people in the world used to know. But I laid it all out there for you. Will you be just as authentic and candid with me? No one else is around. No one is listening. It's just you and me, and I'm on the other side of a book, so it's completely safe.

Are you talking smack to yourself? Do you say and believe the worst about yourself? Are you held hostage to an understanding of your past that has made it impossible to leave it behind?

Finding professional help is not shameful. It is not admitting failure. You need to find a trustworthy source you can confide in, someone who will speak life into you. Maybe you've surrounded yourself with people who aren't improving themselves, feeding the negativity and darkness that's drowning you.

You need someone who truly speaks life, not someone who just nods along and lets you wallow in your misery. Someone who speaks the kind of life and truth that can only come from God, the kind that changes hearts and minds and lives.

Because be honest: Are you speaking life or death over yourself?

Try speaking life over yourself for a day or two and see how it feels. It's not easy to do if you have a habit of speaking death. It'll feel strange at first, like you're lying to yourself. The enemy and the cues from the world will certainly make you think that's the case. But that feeling will let you know right away that you've made a habit of speaking death, not life.

So do it anyway. Pay attention to how you react when life throws curveballs at you throughout the day. Choose to turn surprises (even spilled coffee!) into an unexpected good thing. Build a new habit, one where you speak life instead of death.

God created you. You are worth life.

> *It felt like breathing for the first time after holding my breath for years.*

CHAPTER 5

Stuck Like Chuck

If you shot an arrow into the Texan sky and watched as it soared up and then dropped down into the middle of nowhere, the soil it would pierce was where Tiffany and I used to live.

I'm talking way, way back in the sticks, at the end of a long country road you'd expect to see on *Texas Chainsaw Massacre*, which is a movie you should not see for many reasons, among them because you'll never go down a long country road ever again. The country road we lived on shaved off about 15 minutes of time to get to Terrell, Texas, a faster route than if you went on the blacktop. Save some time, have terrifying nightmares—so many choices.

This was during the time I was back in college, following Payton's diagnosis and our pause from youth ministry. We were pretty busy with doctor's appointments and therapy for Payton, all while I was working full-time as a data-entry clerk. But, without youth ministry included in the mix, life was no longer fulfilling. I wanted to do more.

Since I loved helping young people and I also loved sports, I thought coaching might be a good fit for me. I would go to work during the day and do classes in the evenings. I got mighty familiar with that country road, driving to and from community college in Terrell. However, Tiffany and I didn't see each other very much during this time.

One night, I was running late for class. The entire week had been filled with nonstop rain, and I knew that the country road would be a mud trap, gouged with deep tire ruts from trucks that could get through because they had four-wheel drive. The blacktop was the obvious choice.

But I could save fifteen minutes if I took the dirt road.

I sat at the stop sign for about thirty seconds, debating whether I should stay on the blacktop or turn onto a route which would lead me to the dirt road.

When you're short on time, you also take shortcuts in your decision making. I didn't want to be late for class. I knew what I probably should have done, but there's a reason Las Vegas is so popular: we forget the house always wins. So, the shortcut won out. I'd made it before when it was kind of muddy. I was going to be driving a truck. Sure, it didn't have four-wheel drive, but that was overrated.

I'm gonna go for it, I decided. I rolled the dice and turned the wheel to take the shortcut.

By the time I got onto the dirt road—a misnomer at this point, since I would describe it more accurately as a long ribbon of soul-sucking mud— it was too late. Once you commit, you gotta go. The road was narrow; you couldn't turn around, and you had to keep your momentum up. It was necessary to find a way to flaunt physics and go fast enough to hover above the mud. But it was only a mile stretch before you hit blacktop again. How bad could it be?

I gripped the wheel and navigated the deep tire trenches cut into the road, sliding into half of them despite the steering wheel telling the truck otherwise. Suddenly, all that momentum and mud whipped my truck about, and I was spinning out of control. I couldn't stop. Down into the ditch I went, where, if you can believe it, there was more mud than there was on the road.

I couldn't go forward. I couldn't go backward. I was stuck. The truck was stuck. No, the truck was *buried*. It was kind of phenomenal, really, until I hopped out of the truck and felt myself sinking into the mud as well.

By now, it was very dark. It was scary because remember: long country roads and horror movies. Some redneck was going to take my head for a trophy and put it on a fence post. Every noise was either a guy with a monstrous bladed tool or the chupacabra.

I'm not even going to tell you the delights of walking in thick mud when it comes to the shoes you're wearing (and then suddenly aren't). One sloppy step at a time, I pressed on. This was quite a shortcut. Shaved off fifteen minutes and added hours.

What am I going to tell Tiffany? I thought. *She's going to be so mad at me. Or laugh. Mad would be better, maybe. We don't have the money to get this truck pulled out of the mud, and now I'll miss class.*

After a while with these kinds of thoughts, the redneck didn't seem so bad.

I made it back to the house. Tiffany and I are still married, so rest easy on that. But the problem of getting the truck out was still real. I tried to get a friend to help me. But he didn't want to bury his truck in the mud either, and I couldn't fault him. I ended up shelling out $350 to a guy with what seemed like a tank on tracks. Once he got my truck out, he looked up and down the road, and then back at me.

"What were you thinking?"

Well, I wasn't. That much was clear.

I handed the guy the money but didn't say anything to him. I said plenty to myself, though. I felt so stupid. What a huge, expensive mistake. I was positive that no one in the history of the world had ever spent thirty seconds in front of a stop sign only to make the dumbest decision available. That was me speaking negatively to myself.

Stupid stupid stupid. How could you be so stupid? I was stuck in a different kind of mud.

We All Get Stuck, in Everything

Have you ever felt stuck?

We get stuck in our health, our career, our spiritual walk, our relationships—everything that matters. You hit a wall, and you can't get past it. You do everything you can think of, but that needle on the scale won't move. You promise you're going to stick to a Bible reading plan, and then you hit Leviticus. You vow to be a prayer warrior but crumble when it seems your prayers are stuck to the ceiling. You go to work and see a career of zero opportunity for advancement or professional development stretch out before you endlessly, certain there's no room for growth. Your pie-in-the-sky dreams for your marriage ended up more like mud pies, and you're tired of the arguing.

Stuck.

I know it well.

This book, for example. I'm writing, I'm writing, the words are flowing, and then the doubts creep in and I start to think I can't do this. I don't have enough material for a book. No one wants to hear my story. No one is going to read this. I'm a fool for thinking I should do this.

Stuck is being paralyzed in your own self-doubt.

But God is really good at whispering to us above the noise of the grinding of gears and spinning tires, the mud flying all around us. He interrupted my self-doubts by suggesting that He allowed the feeling of being stuck to happen so I can help other people. It didn't happen to me, but it happened for me.

I happen to know that people get stuck much worse than I did that night in the mud. It's interesting to pay attention to what happens not just to them, but to those around them.

> ## *Stuck is being paralyzed in your own self-doubt.*

As I write this chapter, there is a huge cargo ship jamming up the Suez Canal right now. Not only is being stuck a problem for its crew, but for all of the other ships behind it who can't get past. Hey, captain, I feel for you. Come to Texas sometime when it's raining.

And do you know the story of baby Jessica? She was the baby who fell down the well in West Texas and became horribly stuck. Even though there was no internet or social media back then, her story went viral. I was only eight, but I remember that every news channel and newspaper shared updates on her rescue. It took days for teams to get to her, and they eventually saved her life. My whole family was glued to the television, eager to hear the updates. Like many Americans, we'd been praying for the family and for baby Jessica. She lives a normal life today, even though she was stuck and nearly died.

When someone gets stuck, it affects people around them, too.

There are lots of ways to get stuck. Bad decisions, accidents—even just doing daily life. And then suddenly, no more movement. Nowhere to go. No way to get out.

At least, that's how it *seems* at the moment. What you need is a release mechanism. You need to cut the rope.

Cut the Rope

In 1853, there were only a few buildings in New York City that were taller than five stories. The reason for that is far less dramatic than you'd imagine: people simply didn't want to climb more than five flights of stairs. I can't blame them. But then a man named Elisha Otis had an idea that would change the world.

He'd been working in a Yonkers, New York bedstead factory, and that required moving heavy machinery between floors. He was concerned about what would happen if the support rope on the equipment elevator broke, so he devised a "safety hoist" to fix the problem. The hoist was a device made of a steel wagon-spring and a ratchet that made sure that, should the rope give way, the spring would catch and keep the platform from plummeting down and crushing everything below. Nothing like that existed until Otis came up with the device, since elevators weren't used for much more than equipment.

But no one would believe his device could be trusted for use with people. Like most great ideas, they are seen as crazy and unthinkable ideas before they are seen as great ideas.

Otis needed to demonstrate his idea, and he found the perfect moment at the 1854 New York World's Fair. There on the stage, perched high above the gasping crowd in a makeshift elevator, he proved his idea in the most dramatic way possible.

He cut the rope.

If his brake didn't work, he'd plummet to his death in front of the audience. He might even hurt onlookers. But it worked. By 1908, there were 538 skyscrapers in New York City, and it's been said that the Otis Elevator Company moves the entire population of the earth every three days. In New York City alone, more than three million people ride in his elevators.

I'm guessing Otis had some moments of significant fear during the whole process. Fear that he was wrong, fear that no one would listen, fear that his idea would fail. But despite all the people telling him no, he didn't stay stuck. He saw the safety rope as the barrier between him and success, and he cut the rope.

I've been stuck in every way possible. In life. In my marriage. In my health. In my walk with God. Some days, I've been nearly stuck in bed, barely able to get up and face the day. It felt overwhelmingly impossible to overcome every moment of being stuck, but I'll tell you: there is hope.

Once upon a time, there was a widow. Her husband had loved the Lord, but he was gone. She was on her own with just her two sons and lots of debt. One day, a man of God—a prophet—came by. His name was Elisha.

"My husband is dead!" she cried out to that prophet. "You know he loved the Lord. But now his creditors are coming. I have nothing to give them. Nothing! They're going to take my two sons as slaves in payment."

"What do you have that we can sell?" he asked her.

"What part of 'I have nothing' didn't you understand?" (I'm paraphrasing a bit here.)

"Surely you have something."

"I'm stuck! All I have is a jar with some olive oil in it."

Now, picture her position. She's going to attempt to barter for the lives of her children with a ceramic jar of olive oil? I can't even begin to imagine her level of fear and desperation.

"We're good," Elisha told her. "That's all you need. Go around and ask your neighbors for empty jars."

She looked at him, maybe a little frustrated, thinking he was missing the picture.

"Don't ask for just a few. Seriously, get as many as you can. We need a lot," he continued. "Then, get them all together, and pour your oil into the jars. Once one is full, set it aside."

I have no idea what that widow was thinking while she obeyed Elisha. Maybe she felt a bit like Elisha Otis, dangling high above the ground, holding onto her last thread with her own Elisha reaching for the scissors. Maybe she wondered about his grasp of the situation. Who knows? The point is that she did what he told her to do and poured her oil into the first jar she'd gathered. Then, it was full, and so she poured into another. And another. And another. She asked her sons to get more jars, but pretty soon, they had all the jars they could scrounge up, and everything was full. At that point, the oil stopped flowing.

"There you go," Elisha said. "You can go sell the oil and pay off your debts. You and your sons can live off of the rest."

This story can be found in 2 Kings, and it's a true story of how amazing God is. No matter how stuck you are, He'll provide for you even when things seem impossibly precarious. Over and over, we see in His Word how He provides for people precisely as they need, in the moment they are stuck.

Cain and Abel, for instance. Yes, I know we think of that more as a murder story, but let's look at Genesis 4 a bit differently. Cain was a farmer, and Abel was a shepherd. The two brothers made sacrifices to God, each from what he had produced, but God favored Abel's sacrifice over Cain's.

So, Cain killed his brother. That was his solution.

Why did God favor Abel's sacrifice instead of Cain's? Did he not like grain? No, it was because Cain sacrificed out of obligation, while Abel sacrificed out of love for the Lord. And when I was stuck writing this very chapter, my life coach, Dave, reminded me of that story.

"Fall in love with your calling," he told me.

I'm called to write. I'm called to help and serve people. When I have good intentions but can't write, I justify excuses that keep me from reaching a goal. I start moving from love into obligation. I get stuck in a rut.

You know what a rut is? It's simply a grave with the two ends kicked out of it.

I now ask God to accept my sacrifices. There are a lot of things that keep me from writing. Some are good things, like taking my daughter to a doctor's appointment. But some aren't valid reasons. I want to be able to sit down to write and ask the Lord to accept my sacrifices, to partner with me and help me fulfill my calling for His Glory.

Dave often reminds me that God can't drive a parked car; you have to be in action for God to use you. You can't prove your elevator brake will work unless you have an elevator on the move. Dave's son, Paul, a genius in his own right, says that it's the "other things" that keep us from reaching our full potential. We tend to avoid the very things that would make us better because, for whatever reason, they're distasteful to us. We want the full reward but don't want to pay the price. We want to look fit but don't want to work out. We want the degree but don't want to go to class.

You get it. You can't skip the hard work and get the same results.

Maybe you've been praying for your spouse to return to the passionate relationship you had at the beginning. But, for some reason, you skip all the intentional ways of loving them along the way and just expect to wake up one morning to an amazing marriage. We've had people come to us and tell us they want the successful business that we have. I believe anyone could do the work and get there. It takes a lot of hard work, but not everyone will put it in. They know what they want; they just don't like the path it takes to get there.

There's a difference between what comes from obligation and what comes from love.

How To Get Out of The Bermuda Triangle

We used to live just south of Lake Okeechobee, which is the largest freshwater lake in the state of Florida. There are fishing tournaments there all the time, and all the big sports networks come over to cover them.

I guess there are a few fish in the lake. I wouldn't know. I might be from the country, but I'm not into fishing. Our church had several professional fishermen who attended services, though, and one decided I needed to go fishing with him.

"This will be fun," he assured me.

I figured he was right.

"I'll pick you up at 4 a.m."

Strike one.

I barely remember getting out of bed that morning, and on the way to the lake, we had to stop to pick up my fishing license. It cost me $60.

Strike two.

We made it to the marina and had a good breakfast. That was probably the best part of the day, now that I look back. Before we dropped the boat into the water, he suggested we leave our cell phones in the truck.

You can't skip the hard work and get the same results.

"The best part of fishing is being alone with God, on the water, without distractions."

OK . . . though we could've just turned our phones off. But he was the expert, so that was what we did.

Soon, we were in the boat and flying across the water. His new boat was amazing, and the cool morning air felt great. The sun was just starting to come up, and we had this massive lake almost to ourselves. It was gorgeous.

Once we got to his favorite spot, he showed me how to cast, and I got the hang of it. For forty-five minutes, we cast and then reeled in. Nothing. But I was enjoying myself, so I didn't pay attention to the time.

"I have a better spot," he said, reeling his line in. "Let's go try there."

Across the lake we went, a twenty or thirty minute ride. Then we started casting again. Nothing.

A few of his buddies came by in their boat, holding up two lines of what looked like ten or twelve big fish. They hollered and waved.

"Where were you at?" my new fisherman friend asked.

"Just a bit up around the bend," they told him.

He got excited, and we quickly reeled in before taking off for the new spot, screaming like a couple of junior high girls at all the fish we'd soon be catching.

After 10 minutes of casting and reeling, it happened.

My friend snagged a big fish, and I watched as he masterfully worked the line. His rod was nearly bent in half as he was trying to reel it in, but suddenly, the fish jerked his rod out of his hand.

"Quick! Give me your rod!" he screamed at me. I gave it to him, and he tried to use it to hook his old rod, which was fast disappearing under the water. It wasn't working. He grabbed his anchor and threw it overboard, hoping to catch the rod. He pulled the rope up, and I realized there was no anchor on the end.

He hadn't tied his anchor to the rope.

I sat there very quietly, unsure of what the proper response was since fishing was new to me. What do you do in moments like these? What did fishing etiquette dictate I should do? It was the closest real-life Jonah moment I'd ever had, because he seemed pretty upset and I thought he might throw me overboard.

Things on the boat were silent for a bit, just the sound of the lake water slapping the side of the boat.

"Man. That was a $100 rod and reel," he said.

Probably not the time to remind him I, too, had experienced monetary loss earlier when I paid $60 for my fishing license. We sat there in silence for a couple more minutes. I could feel him processing the great loss he'd just experienced.

"You know, Pastor Andy," he said. "I think we need to go. I'll bring you back another day."

I nodded. "This has been so much fun, but I completely understand. We can go."

I was a bit relieved until he went to start his boat. His brand-new, beautiful boat that had been flying all over the lake not that long ago would not start. Over and over, he tried.

"No biggie," he said, staying calm. "My boat has a trolling motor. It's not as fast, but it'll get us back."

He shifted over to get the trolling motor in place, but the brackets that held it snapped off, and the motor began to sink in the water. He leapt forward to grab it, barely staying in the boat himself, but he did manage to pull it onboard. It was starting to feel like one of those Bill Dance fishing blooper videos, but I just sat quietly because these kinds of things are funny later. Much later.

He buried his face in his hands.

I have never felt more awkward or scared to move in my life. A boat is a small place. You can't just leave the room and let a man be alone. I later learned the man was a new Christian, so I'm surprised he didn't start swearing in front of me. He was actually pretty calm, considering.

I did notice that we were drifting, though, and I wasn't sure what to say. Soon, we were up at the shoreline, hitting the rocks.

"No! Not my paint job!"

I felt terrible. You could hear the rocks scraping his new boat. It sure would've been nice to have a phone right about then. It was just us, peacefully with God and the rocks.

Eventually, the same buddy with all the fish came by and saw us. He was able to use the anchorless rope to pull us to shore. We got his boat back on the trailer.

"I want to try to start it, just one more time," he said to me. Sure enough, the engine roared to life.

He just looked down and shook his head. Then he looked at me. "We must have been in the Bermuda Triangle or something."

Every day all over, people are getting stuck. I've been there. The captain of a huge cargo ship has been there. We get out, but it's very likely we'll get stuck again someday. So, when you're adrift, unable to move, with mocking fish all around you, just remember a few things:

1. **Breathe.** To quote the great quarterback Aaron Rodgers . . . R-E-L-A-X. It will be OK. The worst thing you can do if you're stuck in quicksand is thrash about in a panic. Back float—not front—your way out, and don't backstroke your way out. Small, controlled movements, close to your core, to keep the quicksand from getting more liquefied. A quick fix, like a shortcut on a muddy dark country road, puts you in serious trouble.

2. **Spit.** Hear me out; I learned this on a TV show about rescues. Let's say you're caught in an avalanche. What you should do is spit. Watch where it goes. If you don't get hit in the face by your own spit due to gravity, you have an idea of where to climb. You lose your sense of direction when you're stuck in an avalanche. There's noise and chaos, and all around you is white snow. Many people who have died in an avalanche were found crawling in the wrong direction. Figure out which way is forward so you know the right direction to go to get unstuck.

3. **Lean.** When I'm stuck, it's hard to lean on others and tell them my secrets. I had to open up about my depression, even though it made me feel weak. Pretty soon, though, I saw the benefit of

leaning on others, and today I have a life coach I can bounce things off of to prevent myself from going backward. It's OK to ask for help.

4. **Trust.** I don't know where you are in your faith; but if you don't know Jesus, I don't know how you're doing it. Life is seriously hard, and I have to put my trust and hope in Jesus. I trust that He will do the part He's promised. The Bible tells us the Lord loves even the sparrows, so how much more must He love us? He didn't create you to watch you get stuck and die. I wake up each day and partner with God by trusting Him.

5. **Go.** If you're in a rut, you gotta get into action. One of the reasons I like working out is that if I didn't, you'd realize I was a jerk. Moving, working up a sweat, making my body go—I feel better. All those endorphins that your brain releases when you're moving make a huge difference. If you don't get into action, you get the same results you've always had; that's not helpful if you're stuck. Try something new. Even if it doesn't work out, the action of trying has benefits. While I know God blessed our business, we put a lot of effort into it. I think God was pleased, and that was why He blessed it.

6. **KISS.** It's the classic old acronym: Keep It Simple, Stupid. Ha. No, I'm not calling you stupid. But if you're like me and get overwhelmed very easily thinking you have to fix every aspect of your life, you'd appreciate the acronym. Instead of taking on everything, focus on one area at a time. It's like the old saying "how do you eat an elephant?" You eat it one bite at a time. Tiffany has an exercise that helps with this: get index cards and write on them the areas in your life where you feel stuck. Finances, relationships, health, career, parenting—whatever comes to mind. Pull one index card out at a time, and focus on that. Go through steps 1–5, and make the new habits you need to make for that index card. Once you're ready, grab another card. If you try to do everything all at once, you'll feel burned out and overwhelmed and . . . you guessed it . . . *stuck.*

There are so many amazing resources available today to help you in just about any area you might be stuck. The internet is full of videos, podcasts, blogs, and books. (They will even read those books to you these days with audiobooks, can you believe it.)

> *The only thing holding you back is you.*

The only thing holding you back is you. Anything is possible. It's true, and that's what I want you to understand. Tiffany and I are living proof that everyone gets stuck deep in the mud at some point, and that you can get unstuck, too.

CHAPTER 6

Bring On Goliath!

I've always felt like I had to prove something to the world. Like there's some cosmic roller coaster sign that reads: "You must be this tall to ride," only I can never quite measure up to that line. Have you ever felt like this? As if no matter how much you accomplish, it's never enough . . . No matter how hard you try, it's never enough . . . No matter how much you want to be worthy, *you* are never enough . . .

The crazy thing is, that feeling isn't true for me (or for you). It's a lie, a sinister lie that works itself down deep into our minds because it's straight from the first liar: the enemy. The truth is, you and I never had anything to prove.

My parents loved me unconditionally, the way only a parent can. They worked their fingers to the bone to provide for us. And what we didn't have in "stuff," they more than made up for in love, time, and prayer. Somehow, each of us kids always felt like number one. I can also tell you they never missed a single event of ours. Which is impressive, because there were a lot. I remember one in particular because I was playing a role in a one-act play for our school. And this was the kind of thing that was waaaay out of my dad's comfort zone. However, he loved me. I landed a part. So, when the curtains opened: boom. There he was, front and center, right next to my mom. Their love and support always meant the world to me and still does.

So why would I feel like I had to prove my worth? Because no matter what my parents did or said, there was a lie that whispered doubts, and I believed them, little by little. I felt like a broken picture in a dark room, while my brothers—my absolute heroes—were the main events, the real giants of my family.

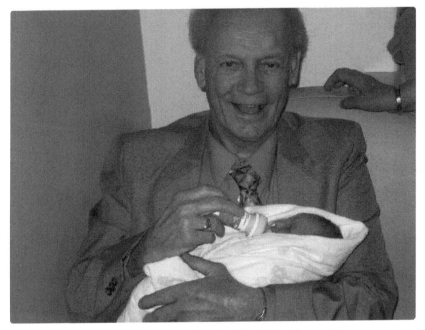

My Dad and Payton. There's nothing like the love of a parent!

I love my older brothers, and I've always looked up to them because you tend to look up at giants, you know? Giants in their faith. Giants in the community. Giants in musical talent. Giants in high school sports, church sports, college sports . . . all the sports.

I was a few years behind all of them, meaning I didn't always get to be a part of the things they were doing. My brother Keith's bachelor party was the guys playing basketball. I'd have killed to be a part of it, but I was nine years old and short and got stuck with mom and dad. My brother Jamie could hit and field a softball like no one else. My brother Mo had an amazing baseball career and even tried out for some professional teams, but he chose to follow God's call into ministry instead of playing pro ball. And my brother Tim always impressed me the most by how easy he performed in front of people. He was always himself and never ashamed or shy of it. It makes sense that he would chase his dreams and become a DJ and work radio airwaves for more than twenty-five years.

My brothers weren't just great at sports—they were great at being human beings in general. Great sense of humor, great at telling jokes, great musicians. They went from instrument to instrument and played them all like a master. But it's their love for God and for serving people that has always impressed me the most, much more than some sports statistics. Each of my brothers ended up pastoring churches and are still in the ministry today. I marvel when I see how they connect people to God.

I was the baby of the family. People gave me the nickname "little Andy." They didn't mean any harm by it, but after hearing people wonder where little Andy was at, or what little Andy was up to—even when I wasn't so little—it got in my head a bit.

Years later, I took some personality tests. Different tests measure different traits, and then they arrive at your personality type. There's the Myers-Briggs, Ned Herrmann's Whole Brain, DiSC assessment, the Enneagram, the Smalley Trent personality test—depending on the test you take, you might be a number, a color, a combination of letters, or even an animal.

Brace yourself, because apparently, I'm a dog.

When You're in the Doghouse

To be more specific, I'm a golden retriever. Didn't know you were reading a book written by a dog, did you?

According to the personality system devised by Gary Smalley and Dr. John Trent, which divides people into four animal types, I'm a calm, loyal person who avoids confrontation and doesn't make a lot of demands. I like routine and am warm and relational with a dry sense of humor and thoughtful tendencies. I also give in to others easily, don't like change, am indecisive and overly accommodating, and am willing to sacrifice results just to keep the peace.

Golden retriever types tend to stay in a rut and are easily hurt. It's as if you had to choose between a guard dog who would keep the intruders out, or a dog who would, with the promise of a treat or pat on the head, show them where the gold is stashed.

With that personality test, if you weren't a golden retriever, you could be a lion, an otter, or a beaver. And while being a dog sounds way better than being an otter or beaver, I've struggled with my personality my whole life. When my wife and family took that test, I discovered I was surrounded by strong lions and fun-loving party-time otters, and it only made me feel worse.

"Andy, dude, your family sounds great. And they love you. What's the deal?" you might wonder.

I get it. But it's a piece of the puzzle when it comes to understanding my story. I was an accommodating golden retriever living in the shadows of overachieving giants. That hurt.

> *I was an accommodating golden retriever living in the shadows of overachieving giants.*

For years, I used Payton and everything that had happened with her as the source of my pain. It made sense to other people, they were sympathetic, and it was an easy out for me. In a way, I even thought that was the culprit for all of it. The challenges that situation created were the justification for how I responded to them, the way I tried to mask pain through food or other things.

But the real culprit was self-doubt.

Maybe being called "little Andy" had a cumulative effect. Maybe I just spent too much time listening to the voices in my head telling me I could never live up to my brothers. But if we operate on the idea that God intentionally made us, and that he knew what he was doing, then that lack of confidence I had in myself was also a vote of no confidence in God. Whatever the case, I allowed—heck, I fed—my self-doubt to grow into a massive monster. I let it mock me, call me out, and keep me from moving into the destiny God had created me for. Self-doubt was my Goliath.

People like to make fun of Moses for wandering around in the desert for forty years. Leave it to a man to wander for forty years and not ask for directions, right? Yet while God uses the number forty in the Bible to signify testing and trial, today we use the number forty as the cutoff date for usefulness. It's as if we all have sell-by dates that end at age forty. We have forty-under-forty lists to celebrate the success of youth. Birthday decorations for when you turn forty are almost like funeral arrangements.

But Moses's greatest years came after age forty. There's no shortage of people whose greatest years came after age forty, from Ronald Reagan to Sam Walton to Julia Child to Colonel Sanders. I tell you that because I have to remind myself of that, too. It feels like I was dragging around for most of my life until I flipped the switch at age forty; it seems to me that my best years are ahead of me, but those whispers in my head would like to say otherwise.

You know what happens before age forty? No, I'm not talking about what happens to your knees and joints. That's a different book. What happens before you turn forty is that you get to experience a lot of hard life lessons that you can use to help so many people.

I might be an aging golden retriever, but I have a lot of good years ahead of me because God's timeline and plan for our lives isn't as limited as the world would have us believe. The lead-up to this realization, however, was rough.

The Voices from the Sidelines

In seventh grade, most of my focus on the basketball court was on how to not screw up instead of how to get better. I had talent but no confidence, and that was the form it took.

That's a self-help book you should avoid, one on how not to screw up. When you have that kind of twisted focus, it's all about self-restriction. Don't extend, don't try, don't take a chance, color within the lines, and only do what you know for sure is safe. You won't discover anything new, but you won't screw up either. That's tough enough for an adult, but imagine being a seventh grader out on the court with two big brothers in the stands, hollering suggestions.

"Andy, you have to be more aggressive!" they'd tell me. "You have five fouls. Use some."

Golden retrievers don't get fouls because that's breaking the rules and causing problems. I don't think I hardly used a foul, ever.

"Go after the ball, Andy! Just go get it!" they'd yell.

This distressing routine culminated into a big game where my brothers began putting the pressure on me. Publicly. It was the last quarter, and I'd put zero points on the board, with my one big moment being an accidental rebound.

"Foul! Foul!" I heard my brothers yelling from the stands as I ran back and forth. "C'mon! Foul!"

Being twelve was awkward enough; you can barely run without tripping on your own feet. But I was overly tall for my age, so watching me move up and down the court was like watching the circus arrive in town. And now my brothers, mighty basketball players of renown, were embarrassing me. It was incredibly confusing, what with my feet not obeying the instructions my brain was sending, the pressure to not mess up, and my brothers yelling for me to intentionally foul.

"What are you doing, Mo?!" the coach yelled at me, cuing in on the on-court confusion.

Mo? I mean, why not. Why not add to the horror and pubescent chaos of the moment and have my coach start hollering out my brother's name? Was he yelling at my brother? Was my brother's name the only name my coach had room for in his head? I think it was the latter, frankly, because every time he coached a sibling, he called the kid by the name of the first sibling he'd ever coached.

As all this yelling and contemplation of coaching philosophy was mulling in my head, as I tried to march to the beat of a drummer meant for Mo, it happened.

One of the players on the opposing team was dribbling the ball. He was ten city blocks from the basket, and we were in the back court. That was when I made my strategic move.

I just grabbed the dude.

As in, full-on bear hug, which was followed by the ref's whistle. I had accomplished nothing for no one, but I thought that was what my brothers had wanted me to do.

Whew. I fouled. My brothers will be so proud of me, I thought.

"Matt, go in for Mo!" I heard the coach yelling from the sideline as a teammate stood up from the bench. Fine with me. I shrugged my shoulders and ran to the bench, partly wondering if Matt was going to take Mo's spot in the stands because my name was Andy. Little Andy.

My brothers later informed me that they didn't necessarily want me to foul, but to not be afraid to foul. They wanted me to be more aggressive by putting on defensive pressure or getting the ball, not just give some guy a hug. Hugs are nice, but not during the game. The other team got two free throws, I got more time on the bench, and the coach thought negative things about Mo.

The view from the sideline gives context for the voices that come from there. Theodore Roosevelt gave a famous speech in Paris in 1910, one people have come to call "The Man in the Arena."[4] Originally entitled "Citizenship in a Republic," one paragraph was powerful enough to draw all the attention and change how it's known:

> *It is not the critic who counts; not the man who points out how the strong man stumbles or where the doer of deeds could have done them better. The credit belongs to the man who is actually in the arena, whose face is marred by dust and sweat and blood; who strives valiantly; who errs, who comes short again and again, because there is no effort without error and shortcoming; but who does actually strive to do the deeds; who knows the great enthusiasms, the great devotions; who spends himself in a worthy cause; who at the best knows in the end the triumph of high achievement, and who at the worst, if he fails, at least fails while daring greatly, so that his place shall never be with those cold and timid souls who neither know victory nor defeat.*

When you're twelve, you don't understand anything like that. You see the crowd, you hear the yelling, and you stumble. You'd like to think you get your act together by the time you're an adult. But when you have no self-confidence and are wrapped in self-doubt, you listen to the critic. There are a lot of voices hollering at you from the sidelines. They might even have some good advice. But when you're the man in the arena, you have to be careful who you listen to.

They should definitely at least get your name right.

Goliath the Mocker, King of Second Sandwiches

I was always a two-sandwich kid. I noticed other kids would have just one, but I always went for the repeat performance.

I didn't think too much about it back then. When you're young and active in sports, you have spectacular metabolism and everything's golden. You can have candy bars and potatoes and pizza as your main food groups, chase it down with a Coke, and get away with it. Then, as you

---

4   Roosevelt, Theodore. *"The Man in the Arena." TR Center – Man in the Arena. Accessed April 6, 2022. https://www.theodorerooseveltcenter.org/Learn-About-TR/TR-Encyclopedia/Culture-and-Society/Man-in-the-Arena.aspx.*

get older, when you're less active, you still turn to the comfort food that didn't seem to harm you when you were young.

Funny thing about comfort food. It silences pain for a short, short while, yet builds some new pain that crushes you down the road. It absolutely makes your life uncomfortable.

I come from an amazing family with not only incredible gifts and talents, but type 2 diabetes, heart disease, and morbid obesity. As I write this, I get a sense of incredible loss when I think of how many people I loved died way too early, people I would love to help today with the tools I've adopted in my own life that are now helping thousands of others.

Goliath stood in the valley between me and my destiny, a giant of self-doubt, but I never thought he'd start off as a sandwich. The thing about Goliath is that he's not just some big barrier that seems impossible to get past. He's also a mocker, and he sees you coming.

I wasn't long out of my teens before those extra sandwiches and the comfort food caught up to me. At twenty-five, I was having health issues, and my doctor finally sent me to take part in a sleep study.

I got to the clinic around 10 p.m., signed in, and then, as I looked around, realized I was about the only person in the room who was not a member of the AARP. Everyone was old.

What am I doing here? I thought. *This is for old people.*

I had to laugh to keep from crying.

I was shown to the room where I'd sleep, a lab that seems like a bedroom. They needed to monitor what was happening to me while I was sleeping to see if there were issues causing the problem, and so they stuck some gadgets to my body that made me feel like I was in a sci-fi movie.

I'll ace this test, I thought as I drifted off to sleep. *My doctor will see this was a silly idea.*

With a sleep study, you're supposed to spend the night, and then in the morning, they deliver the results with whatever recommendations they had. I was awakened by the doctors at 1 a.m. and told I could go home because they'd seen all they needed to see.

Yeah, I aced it alright.

"You are by far the sickest person at our facility," they said, giving me a temporary BiPAP machine while rushing a personal one to me by next evening. "Do *not* sleep without your BiPAP."

Side note: I was 345 pounds. Simply walking made me sweat profusely and get out of breath. I couldn't even give blood at the local blood drive, denied because of my health. I suppose I knew I was sick, but there's nothing like hearing it from a white coat.

"Hey, fatty, why don't you take me on so I can crush you and feed your fat flesh to the birds?" Goliath said to me. I mean, I don't know if that's exactly how it was said, but that's how I remember it. That voice in my head was harsh, it hurt, and I felt completely hopeless. Sleep apnea, fatty liver, high blood pressure, high cholesterol, borderline diabetic, and probably the next one in my family to die young.

Six months after my dad had died from cancer, my brothers and I were scheduled to lead the worship for a men's conference. My brother Mo was the district worship director, and we thought it would be a good way to honor our dad. It was one of the happiest memories I have, such a precious time to celebrate the Lord, honor my dad, and do it alongside my brothers, who are some of the finest musicians I know. We even took a photo of all of us to commemorate the night, and I still have the photo.

The photo that began my health journey (Tim, Keith, Mo, Jamie, and Me).

There we were, the five Howard boys, four men on the left with me on the right, taking up half the picture. Despite my efforts to wear clothes to hide my weight . . . I was massive.

"Ha! You take up half the picture out of five grown men. Failure!" Goliath said.

I was sick of Goliath. He took one of the best times of my life and tried to destroy it. His mocking echoed endlessly in my head, and I knew it wouldn't end until I did something.

I decided to have surgery and get a gastric sleeve. The good news is that I quickly lost 160 pounds. The bad news is that, along with the fat, I also lost a lot of muscle. Still, I'm thankful. I know without those initial changes in 2011, I wouldn't be here today. In fact, all of those weight-related illnesses I had were gone. I was finally healthy, I thought.

The tricky thing about the surgery solution is that it addresses symptoms, but not the problem. Do you ever watch those weight loss reality TV shows where people get gastric surgery? They identify their problem as their weight, and jump through all the hoops to get the surgery, and then they lose some weight. They seem to be on the right path, seem to have defeated the giant, seem to have tasted victory. But then it starts to unravel again because they thought they had a weight problem when what they had was something more. What they fixed wasn't the real problem.

I silenced Goliath for a while with that weight loss, but he was still standing there. I hadn't actually dealt with Goliath but instead focused on the noise he was making, and so that silence felt like a win. Sure, I was finally at a healthy BMI, but I never got to the heart of the real issue. And that meant in time, I began eating again. A small stomach can grow, and I hadn't changed my eating habits.

In 2015, while at an insurance evaluation for work, I discovered I had to pay a higher premium because of my health.

"Mr. Howard, you gained forty pounds in the last year," the woman from the insurance company said. I couldn't hear the rest of it because Goliath's loud laughter drowned it out.

If I gain another 40 pounds this year, I'll be back in the 300-pound club that I thought I'd left behind. I knew I had to do something about Goliath for real. I had to do more than just shut him up. I had to defeat him.

Going To the Rock

"Take these pills and lose the fat and get rock hard abs, like the Rock!" Or something like that. That was my plan.

OK, so I've always had a man crush on Dwayne "The Rock" Johnson. I mentioned that before. (Hey, I told you I'd be real and transparent, and I gotta put this out there. I'm trusting you to not laugh.)

I love his confidence. His physique. The way he carries himself. How he battled and worked hard and turned seven dollars into millions. He's one of my favorite people on earth, and if it came down to having a chance to have dinner with Dwayne Johnson or Tiffany . . . it would be a very close decision . . . But I think Tiff would understand.

After Goliath resumed mocking me again, I came across an ad in a magazine that showed a pic of Johnson and a bottle of weight loss pills. I can't honestly say I know exactly what they were, but I bought a bunch without giving it a second thought. I was desperate, and the Rock wouldn't do me wrong. Plus, there was a two-week, no-questions-asked return guarantee. How could I lose anything but weight?

First, I don't think the people selling those pills actually knew the Rock, because when the pills arrived and I had second thoughts and decided to not even open them, they asked plenty of questions and were not nearly as friendly as the magazine ad had led me to believe. In the midst of me juggling a man crush and sketchy sales tactics, Tiffany had scoped out the problem and changed our lives forever.

My life coach Dave asked me recently, "Andy, how did you go from a lifelong couch potato to gaining twelve pounds of muscle in a year?" It started with Tiff and me making a decision.

She'd signed us up for a health program because we both agreed that our life and our destiny were too important. We wanted to leave a legacy for our twins and for Payton; and if we didn't make changes, they'd follow in our footsteps and have to face the same challenges with food that we had. We were fixated on our need to lose weight and get healthy.

So, that was what we did.

There was an easy-to-follow plan. Tiffany became my health coach. She dove full-on into the program, learning everything about it, and it became a passion of ours. There was a community to support us and an overall team who wanted to see the world get healthy.

Goliath is kind of like whack-a-mole, though, and even when you're doing well, he likes to pop up and make you question why you're putting in the work. He's the absolute worst because he mocks you both for failure and for trying. So, defeating him doesn't stop with making a decision (something I learned from gastric surgery); you have to understand why you made the decision. If you don't know why you made a decision, you'll fall victim to Goliath's taunts.

A week after we started the healthy life program, we had a birthday party for the twins at Chick-fil-A. Waffle fries and chicken and cupcakes, all flying around us like butterflies, beautiful and tempting . . . but we held each other accountable. I wasn't trying to lose all seventy-eight pounds I'd eventually lose on that one day, but I knew why we were doing this, and I wanted to win that day.

A week later, we had employee appreciation week at work. The first day was apparently all the donuts ever produced in the history of the world, laid out before us. I managed to stagger by and avoid a tragedy, only to have a friend stop by my cubicle with a plate of donuts.

"Have you ever seen so many donuts?" he asked, sprinkles falling to the floor, his face covered in powder. "Don't they look good?"

"Man, get out of here!" I screamed at him. In a puff of powdered sugar, he disappeared. Goliath isn't the only one who can scream, but I was on the edge. I called Tiffany because I was about to cave.

"I can't do this," I told her.

She reminded me of why we were doing it. "We are doing this for the girls. You want to be there to walk them down the aisle. You want to be around to lift Payton when you're in your sixties and seventies," she said. And then she got right to the point. "Everyone eating those donuts will end up fat in three months, and you'll be skinny."

I'm embarrassed to say that while all of her statements rang true to me, her last one did the trick. Super shallow, yes, but super true. I made it through that whole week, not caving on popcorn day, cupcake day, ice cream day, or the big Tex-Mex lunch day. I stayed on the plan 100 percent, and every win birthed new confidence.

By 2019, we were both on a steady path toward health. But then on ESPN I saw something called a Spartan Race. It's a 5K race with over twenty obstacles where, if you couldn't do an obstacle, you had to do thirty burpees. Talk about a mental and physical challenge! My takeaway was that as long as you didn't quit, you won. Simply finishing was a win.

"Tiff, you gotta see this!" I hollered as I ran downstairs. "I'm going to run a Spartan!"

She laughed. I actually laughed, too. But I really wanted to do it. I called my buddy Russ because misery loves company.

"Russ," I said on the phone. "You wanna run a Spartan with me this year?"

He paused, and then said, "Let's do it, buddy."

Later, Russ's wife, Traci, told me that he'd turned down lots of other requests for these kinds of things; but for some reason, he felt he was to say yes to me. I am forever grateful he agreed because Russ kind of looks like the Rock. Shorter, but fearless, and built like a tank. He could roll out of bed and fall into a Spartan Race and win, but I needed to train and get ready.

We bought our tickets that very day, so there was no going back. We were committed.

Me and Russ at my first Spartan Race.

> *If you don't commit,*
> *you settle.*

That was the third step. First, you make the decision, then you come up with why you made that decision, and then you commit.

If you don't commit, you settle. Too many people settle. I don't know if it's the memory of all the losses, or past fears, or the sound of Goliath laughing at you every time you fail. Maybe setting the bar low to avoid all that makes the pain of failure a bit less. I don't know. But can I encourage you to commit to something bigger and greater than you are? So what if you fail? At least you're failing forward. At least you failed trying to make yourself better. As my brothers would say, you gotta be aggressive!

One of the best ways to avoid failing is to stop setting yourself up for failure. A client told me, before going on a fabulous vacation in Hawaii, that she was going to stay on the health plan "as best she could while there."

There's committing to a win and committing to trying; they aren't the same thing. A commitment to try is often permission to fail but counting it as a victory simply because you tried.

"She's already written herself a way out," I told Tiffany. It's not uncommon, people leaving themselves an out, building failure in as an option.

Why did I want Russ to run the race? Because when you surround yourself with people better than you in the area you want to succeed in, you get motivated in a way that doesn't make failure so comfortable. It doesn't make failure an option. When I wanted to learn golf, I found a friend who played college golf. Sure, I humiliated myself out on the course quite a bit and absolutely decimated the grass in the tee box, but that discomfort has spurred me on to get better. My pastor encourages me in my faith. Russ encourages me in my fitness. Dave encourages me as my life coach. Tiffany encourages me in my health. These people—and so many more—all help make me better, help me win or at least fail forward.

One Sunday, my pastor preached a sermon I'll never forget. He loves to use visual illustrations, so you have to remember not to sit too close to the front or ever make eye contact, or you'll find yourself up front and on display. That particular Sunday, I didn't follow my own advice and I found myself up front, with a plastic garbage bag full of trash hanging around my neck. It was a horrible, sour, and dank odor. That was the point.

"Who are you surrounding yourself with?" he asked the congregation, as I stood and marinated in his family's trash. "Do you smell stinky? Or are you better? Do the people in your life make you better, or are they holding you back?"

Think of David from the Bible. He was once a young shepherd, not yet the fierce warrior king. One day, he brought some supplies to the camp where his brothers and the rest of the soldiers were. They were cowering in their camp while there stood gigantic Goliath, mocking the Israelites and, even worse, the one true God.

David could've hung around in the camp with the cowards. He could've let his older brothers define who he'd become.

Instead, he said to Saul, "I can take this dude. I'm not going to wear your armor or use the tools you've assumed I have to use. They're untested. I'm not going to have a fallback for failure."

Your Goliath is that huge, terrifying pain you carry around that prevents you from reaching your destiny. You could walk into the camp and surround yourself with people unwilling to fight their own Goliath, making a "normal" life out of cowering and excuses to justify failure; or you can do what David did.

"I'm not going to let this bum trash talk God," David said, even as others laughed. They didn't know he'd fought off lions as a shepherd. They didn't realize this wasn't his first battle, even if it was his biggest.

David picked up those stones. He put one in his slingshot, took aim, gave it a whirl, and dropped that beast. Then, he took Goliath's own sword and lopped off his head. No more mocking from him.

Why lop off the head?

Have you ever thought that you'd killed your Goliath, only to have him pop up again as negative self-talk and self-hatred? We've all seen enough movies to know that the bad guy is never dead until he's for sure dead. You take off the head.

This is the tricky part, taking off the head.

You just grabbed fast food and you call yourself a health coach?

Wham. Lop off the head. Because 100 percent perfection isn't how to defeat Goliath. No, chasing after perfection is how you give Goliath a foothold in your life. Your pursuit of perfection is where he bases his mockery. Victory isn't my ability to never let a waffle fry cross my lips for the rest of my life; victory was resolving the pain that caused me to want to eat comfort food. I had to deal with the pain of self-doubt and cut off the head once and for all.

Gastric bypass may have knocked my Goliath down, but I still had to take off the head, and that meant doing hard things. Training for that Spartan Race was hard. I was scared of gyms and trainers and would hop around to different equipment until I hit a wall or got bored. Here's me, a 40-year-old lanky dude without a clue. There were grandmas rocking the equipment better in that gym. Tiffany once again came through and found me a scrawny-looking trainer (sorry) because my self-doubt was still in the way. He was super nice, but honestly, he looked like Kip from *Napoleon Dynamite*.

"So, you want to do a Spartan?" he asked when we met, and I got pretty excited because I was feeling as if I was taking the right steps to make it happen.

"Yes."

"Hey, David!" the scrawny, Kip-looking guy yelled. "I want you to come and meet Andy."

David came around the corner of the gym wall, and my heart sank. He was the epitome of what terrified me about gym trainers. He was huge, and I swear his earlobes had muscles. I looked at Tiff with a sick look on my face, as if to ask if this was some kind of joke.

"Good luck," she said, patting me on the back and walking away.

David put me through the hardest workout of my life, but surprisingly, I didn't die. And he turned out to be a really nice guy who, to this day, is my friend and still trains me. He's one of those people I've surrounded myself with who make me better. My friend David, a giant in his own right, helped me slay Goliath. And here's a secret I learned: when I pay and invest in something, I'm more likely to show up. I never thought I'd be the guy who falls in

Me and my trainer David.

love with working out, but I have. I even get a little bit annoyed when my schedule keeps me from working out. David has even referred to me as an athlete.

So, who are you running from?

What is that pain or doubt that's keeping you from moving forward? Is it Goliath, a giant who mocks you to paralyze you into doing nothing? Or have you been running from your own version of David, the one who could help you slay the giant?

With help from God and from my trainer, David, I'm aggressively confronting my Goliath of self-doubt, working on overcoming it. You could say I go to the Rock each day, pick one up, and take aim. I won't say it's easy, but each day holds the promise of a new, little victory that'll give me more confidence to confront the next day.

From couch surfer to Spartan Racer. Believe me, if I can do it, I know you can, too.

CHAPTER 7

A Flashlight of Hope

So, the past few years have been pretty crazy around the world, amirite?

If ever we needed a glimmer of hope, the 2020s would be it. Isolation, fear, depression, addiction—everything that can destroy human beings—reached critical mass; and the cascading effect has been heartbreaking. While I'd been reading one day that suicide among youth was reaching horrifying new heights, it finally hit home; a senior at my daughter's school took his life just after Christmas.

I wish I could have begged that young man for just a few more minutes of his time. I don't know what we would've talked about. Something, anything, to save his life. But I can't. It's too late. I can't help that young man.

When I think about his suicide and all the others, it hits me harder than you might think. You don't go through a life struggling with depression without having shaken hands with the idea of suicide before.

In 2020, almost 50,000 Americans killed themselves, with 1.2 million others attempting to do so. Each day, 130 people, mostly men, kill themselves, making suicide the 12th leading cause of death in the United States.[5]

I'm 100 percent certain you know someone right now who wants to end their life, who is fighting these kinds of dark thoughts. It might even be you, and if it is, can I have a very candid conversation with you?

---

5   *"Suicide Statistics," American Foundation for Suicide Prevention, accessed February 28, 2022. https://afsp.org/suicide-statistics.*

Can I have those few minutes with you that I didn't get with that young man at my daughter's school?[6]

My life right now is crazy good. I love it. It's better than I'd ever dreamed of. I could have quit a long time ago and never gotten to this point.

Imagine being a sick, miserable, 345-pound human being with almost every chronic disease on the books, someone who doubted his worth and value and ability to do anything. Imagine struggling under incredible financial pressure every single day, where just thinking about making it to the next day was a nightmare.

That was me. That was what we were dealing with. You get to the point where the pros and cons of continuing with life are tipping dangerously into the cons.

> *I could have quit a long time ago and never gotten to this point.*

But God takes weak human beings and orders our steps so that He leads us through if we stick with Him—how He does it, I don't know. The furnace of adversity is so hot but so refining. Sometimes God takes you to a place just to feel the heat, but He will never leave you there for the fire to destroy you.

There, and Back Again

At age twenty-four, Tiffany and I had just gotten married, and we were offered a position in a church across the country. I'm guessing her dad would rather have had us live a bit closer, but we went with twenty hours away instead.

We arrived at the city the church was in to see if we wanted the position.

It was a big church, at least compared to what we were used to. There were over one hundred kids coming to the youth group. There was a

---

6   *If you feel like you don't have a few minutes left in you, and you need to talk to some-one right now, please dial 988, the Suicide and Crisis Lifeline. You can call any time, day or night. It's free and confidential.*

brand-new gym for the students, which was a big deal back then and put you on the who's who list of student ministries. The pastor and church showed us so much love, and they put us up in a nice resort for the weekend of our arrival, paying for our meals. We were shown around what would be our new church and my new office, and it was all so perfect.

After careful prayer, we accepted the position. We were so excited, and it felt almost like instant success. Everything was amazing at first, as new things often are.

Before I go on with the story, I want you to know that I have no doubt it was God's will that we went there. We'd prayed, and I do believe we were doing what God wanted us to as we made that huge move in our life. But just because something is God's will doesn't mean that the warm feeling you have is Him sending you to the beach; it could be Him about to take you through a furnace.

The church provided a truck to help us move out there, and when we arrived, there were about thirty people waiting to help. We barely had to do anything. It seemed like a good start.

But a switch flipped.

That pastor who was so sweet to us when we were considering the position, who had lovingly showed us around the church, turned out to be a jerk. He had a cruel streak in him like I'd never seen before. I'd heard horror stories about pastors like this. But I grew up with my dad (and later, my brothers) as an example of a pastor, and my dad was the kindest, most genuine reflection of Christ you could have. It's a good thing I had that background because, if my only experience with a pastor was the guy at the new church, I probably would've left the ministry altogether.

Six weeks in and that pastor had ground me down to nothing. I called my big brother Tim in desperation; Tim has always been my sounding board, and he was my youth pastor growing up. I knew he'd offer some words of wisdom about the situation.

"How's the new job going?" he asked.

"It's OK," I said, the standard generic response that signals that it's not great but would you help draw it out of me please. And that was what he did. I told him everything. I used many words, probably all the adjectives available, and laid it all out.

And then Tim said something to me that I'll never forget. In three words, he gave me the best possible advice, lifting the most incredible burden from my shoulders and my spirit.

"Just come home," he said.

Wow! For some reason, I hadn't realized that was an option. What would people think of me if I returned home six weeks after leaving? Would I be the biggest failure in Howard family history? Would they think I wasn't cut out to be a youth pastor?

Me and my big brother Tim.

But I didn't care about the answers to those questions. For the first time in six weeks, I had peace. I told Tiffany that I was going to the pastor right away the next morning.

"I'm telling him we're leaving," I said. "I'm telling him that we just don't feel right for this position."

She agreed, even though to this day, she would tell you she never thought I would do it.

The next morning, I walked into the pastor's office and told him what was on my heart, offering a month's notice so that we could leave in good standing and not put the church in a bind.

"You can just walk out of my office, smile at my secretary on the way through, and go out the back door," he said. "I want your stuff out of your house by the end of the day."

No thirty people showed up to help us pack, so I guess the honeymoon was over. We were completely on our own.

I remember those six weeks so well, sometimes framed in wondering why God had us go through it. I remember the pastor calling us fat and pretending he didn't know us at social events when, as newcomers, we knew no one else in the room. Countless other unkind things added up quickly over such a short time period.

I learned more about how to treat people during our time there than anywhere else, and that carried over into my next fifteen years of student ministry. God absolutely used this in our lives. He used it to shape us, and ultimately, He used it to prepare us for something far greater than I had planned. I can't even imagine what it would have been like to be at that church when we got the news about Payton. I can't see that pastor consoling us, helping us, loving us. All the moments with wonderful pastors in the years following those six weeks were all the sweeter having had that bitter experience.

A few months after we had moved back home, my brother Tim called me.

"What was the name of the church you were at?" he asked.

I told him.

"Wow, that's what I thought," he said. "I just read in a magazine article that it was hit by a hurricane."

No one was hurt, but the church was extensively damaged.

I'm not saying God sent the hurricane to get back at the pastor. I'm simply saying I marvel at God's timing, His leading, and His hand on our lives. When we are faithful and in close relationship with Him, we can trust his leading, even if it's through a furnace.

Reading the Last Page First

Think of all the great books out there, the novels and literature people say you have to read. Thick books, with lots of pages and small words, with long, run-on sentences. Really, you could just read a summary of the plot online. Get the CliffsNotes version. Just read the last few pages. Or wait until it comes out as a movie, and then have all the annoying readers tell you that the book was so much better and that you ought to read it. Then you find yourself back at square one.

Truth is, there are no shortcuts.

In every area of our life, we rush. This is a microwave world where the goal is to get from start to finish in as short an amount of time and work as possible. We want to see a finished product now. We want to see a return on our investment now. We want instant respect and a platform. If success doesn't happen in the next five minutes, we give up and try something else.

But that leaves no room for day-to-day wins, the kind of victories that build strength upon strength until you are solid and strong without any weakness from rushing.

"One day doesn't make you, and one day doesn't break you," my trainer, David, tells me all the time. Consistency makes the difference. It took me six months from the start of working out before I saw any significant changes. One night, when I walked by the mirror, I was like wow—*hello there!*

This isn't just about exercise. It's about life in general.

I often think about my girls' wedding days, about how the day will be perfect, and how I'll walk them down the aisle and give them away to an incredible Godly man who they've chosen in their great wisdom. I want the very best for them, but I also know I can't just look to that one day in the future. There are a lot of days from now until then that make up the person they'll be. That time is precious, and my girls and I have to fill it with all the challenges and victories and struggles and painful learning moments. I have to let them get skinned knees and hurt feelings and be there to love them through. I have to be the best dad I can be for the whole journey, not just that day in the future, because it's that journey that results in the amazing day.

The idea that there's beauty in the broken is built on this concept.

If we rush to get to instant success and victory, the broken parts in our lives are just flotsam and jetsam that get in our way. Broken people, broken dreams, broken lives, broken bodies. They just slow us down, right?

But we rush on by, miss all the beauty, and end up with a poor result.

You could plant a seed, nurture the seedling, grow a rose bush, fight off the aphids, prune the bush, and someday end up with a gorgeous rose that smells a tiny bit like Heaven. Or you could just buy some rose-scented air freshener and douse your home in chemicals.

Every bad day builds character. Every furnace experience brings out the pure gold. Every pruning creates health and strength. There are no shortcuts around the trials; if you're going to be empowered, you have to go through them.

But that doesn't mean the pain you're feeling right now isn't real. My heart breaks for you if you think the world would be better if you weren't in it because I've seen the other side of suicide. I know the heartache left

There are no shortcuts around the trials; if you're going to be empowered, you have to go through them.

in parents or siblings. Every life touches so many other lives, even when we think we've been forgotten or don't matter.

If you weren't in this world, I promise you, it would be empty. You were made on purpose, with a purpose, by a God who is purposeful. Your life is meant to touch the lives of others. Your story, as you make it through to the other side of the pain, will help others.

Imagine you're taking a tour in one of those mines or caves that are so deep into the Earth that there is absolutely no natural light. It seems pretty cool to be so far under the surface of the Earth until the guide turns off his light, and you get a sense of just how dark pure darkness can be. You hold up your hand and wiggle your fingers; and while you know your hand is somewhere in front of your face, you can't see it. Nobody moves because nobody knows where to move to. The darkness is so dark, you can almost feel it on your skin. Maybe there's some nervous laughter from others on the tour.

Too many people are stumbling around in the darkness, trying to figure things out on their own. Psalm 119:105 says that God's Word is a lamp for my feet and a light on my path. We can't see the full picture, or even where we're going, without the light He provides.

Then the tour guide flips on his flashlight again, the brilliant white light cutting through the darkness like a saber.

You are so grateful for that flashlight. There's nothing like experiencing true darkness to make you swear to never take light for granted again. The thrill of winning is greater if you've tasted losing. You never know the value of a dollar if you've never been without. It's that strange miracle of being able to find more beauty after you've been broken. It's on the other side where you can finally understand. God used my weight problem to not only change my life, but thousands of others, because I'd been through it and understood.

Anyone who makes it through has a flashlight. I want to shine my flashlight of hope—my story—into a dark and broken world so someone can see it. Maybe that someone is you. Maybe tomorrow or next week or next year, you will be doing the same for someone else.

"Why is God allowing me to be hurt like this? To struggle? Doesn't He care? Can't He just make this all stop right now?" you might be asking.

We've all said that at some point, but when you realize that God never wastes a wound and that His love for you supersedes everything else, you can feel peace deep down in that pit of darkness as God's light shows you the way out. He won't take you out, but He will show you the way.

To really believe this, it's important for you to understand the character of God.

He's a good Father who wants the best for us like I do for my girls. He is love, and not the watered-down, lame version of a conditional love we have here on Earth. No, His love is pure, 100 percent perfect with no strings attached. He'll never abandon you. He'll never demand you be better before you deserve to be loved. He'll never leave you feeling empty. In fact, the only thing He left empty was the tomb He was buried in. He died for you and came back to life for you so all your failures and sins wouldn't get between you and Him.

Don't quit today. Not with all that on your side working for you. Tomorrow is just up ahead, and you don't know what God's light will reveal. Tomorrow could hold the little win you need, the big break that changes everything, the sense of peace to get you through. There is hope.

> *Tomorrow is just up ahead, and you don't know what God's light will reveal.*

Tiffany and I have a fundamental truth in our business: lead from the future, act in the now. Set your goal and reverse engineer it to where you are now. Whenever I'm at a funeral, hearing all the inspiring things the person has accomplished and how loved and missed they are, it reminds me of this way of thinking. What do you want said at your funeral? As long as you are still breathing, you have time to change what people will say. Some people find it odd that this idea motivates me, but it does.

If you're lost or stuck or wandering around in the dark, take my brother's advice. Just go home. Maybe you left the church and decided you'd figure life out on your own. Maybe you walked away from God. Maybe you abandoned family and friends. But home is where there's peace, safety, rest, and hope; you wandered away from home and now feel lost and alone.

I'd like to pray for you right now, whether you're a believer in Jesus Christ or not. It's just a simple prayer, but it could make all the difference.

> *Lord, I ask that you comfort my friend. You know them better than they know themselves. You created them, and Your Word says that a man's days are numbered. You know what the future is ahead of them and how long it is. I know the enemy would love nothing more than to kill, steal, and destroy, but You came so they could have life upon life. Please bring peace to them, right now. Make it a peace that only You can give, the kind that gives them strength to try living one more day to the fullest. Help them find the beauty in the broken and see Your light in all the darkness. We love You and thank You for Your faithfulness. Amen.*

I don't know what story God has written for your life, but don't cut it short. Don't skip ahead or force those last pages. Your story is working out to something beautiful.

CHAPTER 8

Lean into the Pain

Horses aren't like people.

This is not the earthshaking, world-changing information you probably had hoped for when you picked up this book, but hear me out. Horses are into-pain animals.[7] That is, they have a natural tendency to push into pressure or pain. Humans, on the other hand, are avoid-all-pain-at-all-costs critters. We have entire destructive industries that specialize in "helping" people avoid pain. Alcohol, drugs, pornography—it's all about pain avoidance.

It's taken me more than a decade to write this book, and during that time, I've learned that the art of procrastination only improves with age. Rarely are we more creative than in our ability to come up with excuses to do something tomorrow. For every reason I had to write the book, I had 10 reasons not to. But it went beyond simply finding excuses to not write; it was also because I was trying to avoid the pain.

Dave, my life coach, has to get some credit because God used him to help me. He has the gift of being able to pull the best out of me. If he were dumpster diving, he'd emerge with a Rolex watch while everyone else would scrounge up moldy takeout containers.

"This book is going to help a lot of people," Dave told me as I was still in the midst of the struggle. "The enemy knows that, and it's why he's working so hard to keep it in the dark. He doesn't want anyone to read it."

---

7   Monty Roberts, "The Whip in Racing," Monty Roberts Shop, last modified April 30, 2010, https://montyroberts.com/the-whip-in-racing/.

If that's the truth, then this might be the most important chapter of them all, because this is my moment of being like Jacob, wrestling with God. It's the chapter I've feared and dreaded writing the most.

If I am transparent and honest, this one's going to *hurt*.

I don't like confrontation. I don't like peeling back the scab. I don't want to show the world all of the ugly. I don't want to cause hurt for Tiffany or my family by being honest. But I have to. And I will. Together, we are going to lean into the pain.

He's Coming for Us

I've extended the shelf life of pain because I allowed fear into my life.

Annie, a friend of ours who was doing a weekly team training, would know exactly what I was talking about. "Some of you have made fear the CEO of your business," she said. "You opened the door and put out a welcome mat for him. You gave him a desk, and now he's calling the shots. You watch him run your life."

When I was 10 years old, my cousin and I went on a trip with my grandma and her new husband out to his place in central Texas. His house was very remote, and he didn't have a TV or air conditioner there. It was the middle of August, and I swear the house was 120 degrees inside. His solution was to keep every window open with no screens, and we'd pray for a breeze to come through and save us all.

One night, when my cousin and I stayed up until 2 or 3 a.m. to tell stories and joke around with each other, taking advantage of the cool evening air, we noticed a car pull up in the darkness about 150 yards away. What caught our attention was that it made a quick U-turn and parked under a tree, its headlights piercing the darkness.

At first, we didn't think much of it. The light in our room was still on, and we felt safe. It hadn't occurred to us that we were in a house in the middle of nowhere, surrounded by darkness, with the interior lights on; we were practically begging to be noticed.

We noticed the car still sitting there, so our talking died down as we watched it. We whispered about what we thought was going on. We saw cars drive by the parked car, and they would flash their lights at each other.

We were intrigued. Was this some kind of secret code?

This went on for a while, and soon we lost interest and went back to telling silly stories and joking around. That is, until we heard it.

Crunch. Crunch. Crunch.

We went silent.

Crunch. Crunch. Crunch.

Someone was walking to the house, and they were getting closer.

Crunch. Crunch. Crunch.

Each step broke the Texas clay soil and what was left of the brown grass.

Crunch. Crunch. Crunch.

He was coming straight for our window, the only one lit up.

Shannon and I looked at each other, our eyes huge and faces pale white. I could see sweat on his forehead, and I'm sure I was sweating in fear, too. We looked around the room. All we had was a broom and a fire extinguisher. *That's it.*

"I'll spray him in the eyes," I whispered to him. "You hit him with the broom."

What we really wanted to do was run, but the house had a strange floor plan where the two main bedrooms were catty-corner from each other, with a screened porch in between. The only way to get to grandma's room was to expose ourselves to the bad guy.

Crunch. Crunch. Crunch.

By now, the footsteps were so loud, we knew we didn't have much time. I was nearly paralyzed and could taste fear in my mouth. We came up with a different plan.

At the count of three, we took off running as fast as we could, screaming at the top of our lungs for ten yards, to get to the other side. Miraculously, we made it. Grandma's husband wasn't too thrilled, even though we told him what we'd seen and heard. When we got back to our room, we showed him where the car was, except . . . now it was gone.

The next day, we all went outside and took a walk. We saw the deep trench of muddy tracks where the car had been parked by a tree, just like we said. We could see the footprints.

"I told you these boys were right," Grandma said to her husband.

To this day, I have no idea what was going on that night or who was trying to get into the house, but I'll tell you what I do know: fear paralyzes, I'm afraid to write this chapter, and I just bought some time with that story.

But like we did with that guy who was sneaking up to the house, we have to acknowledge fear is present sooner or later. At some point, he's going to get to the window; and, like my friend Annie said, we can let him in and let him ruin our lives, or we can do something about it. We can acknowledge he's there or avoid reality at all costs.

I guess I need to tell you why I'm struggling to tell you about the reality I'd let into my life.

I Can't Get Too Close

Give me a stage in front of a bunch of people rather than one-on-one conversation. Give me South Africa and churches of thousands, with me telling the crowds about Payton, rather than sitting across the table from you over a cup of coffee and having to speak out loud what's going on in my life. I'll take the stadium and the platform any day.

I'd rather be disconnected from the group I'm talking to rather than making eye contact with someone who can pretty much see my soul. My therapist once told me that I have intimacy issues. I'm working on that, but it's still really tough to let people get too close to me.

Our hearts are strange things. There's an inverse correlation between what we think we should do to protect them and what actually makes them healthy. That is, we think that if we wrap them up in bubble wrap and Kevlar and lock them away in a safe wrapped in barbed wire, we'll prevent our hearts from getting hurt. When Proverbs 4:23 tells us to guard our heart, I don't think that's exactly what it means.

Then, that lonely, isolated heart, safe from getting hurt by others, is completely damaged by our self-imposed isolation. The more we try to protect ourselves from hurt and pain, the more we end up hurting our heart and causing pain. Inversely related, and so frustrating.

People who do this (people like me) can share our testimonies and have ninety-nine people tell us it was amazing and life-changing, and then one guy walks up and throws a big wet blanket on it and questions the validity of everything we said. That's the guy we remember for the rest of our days. It's a sort of backward take on the parable of the lost sheep,

The more we try to protect ourselves from hurt and pain, the more we end up hurting our heart and causing pain.

where Jesus leaves the ninety-nine to find the one that was lost. We leave the ninety-nine changed lives and chase after the one who didn't like us to figure out why. Countee Cullen wrote a poem entitled "Incident" where she acknowledges this very thing. She details how, as a young girl, she spent seven wonderful months in Baltimore and saw a lot of great things, but the only thing she remembered as an adult was another child calling her a name.

It's easier to believe and latch onto the bad things someone says to us. When the walls around our hearts are up so high in order to prevent hurt, we remember the things that got through our defenses, don't we? This is how I function, and it's why ministry is so hard.

My friend Leanne has a powerful global ministry, and she describes the word intimacy as "into-me-see." It's scary to let people in, especially in ministry when there are a lot of people who have all kinds of things to say to you. But it's just as dangerous to keep all the people out, to avoid pain at all costs.

Pain avoidance is a huge industry. It's also a huge trap because you avoid one pain only to create many more. Pain avoidance tends toward addiction, and one addiction often goes hand-in-hand with another. And those addictions often create other pain for both the person and everyone around them.

Take pornography, for example. Forty million adults in this country regularly visit porn websites, with 10 percent of all U.S. adults (men and women included) having an addiction to pornography, an addiction that easily leads to depression, anxiety, and substance abuse.[8] One method of avoidance causes pain, which leads to needing another method of avoidance.

Everyone has pain. And in some way, we all find ways to avoid it.

We substitute something for the pain, something like food or alcohol or shopping. Some days it seems like nothing drowns your sorrows like a tub of Bluebell ice cream. Or, in the case of my friends Austin and Monique, or even my nephew Zak, drugs are the go-to method. Some turn to shopping, thinking that buying new things and the rush from getting something new will help the hurt go away.

---

8   *Megan Hull and Anna Pickering, eds., "Pornography Facts and Statistics," The Recovery Village Drug and Alcohol Rehab, last modified June 03, 2022, https://www.therecov-eryvillage.com/process-addiction/porn-addiction/pornography-statistics/.*

You know how I know we live in a world with increasing amounts of pain? Because we live in a world of increasingly unhealthy people, of people in financial disarray. Pain substitutes take a toll on the physical body, on our relationships, and on our bank accounts. Look around you. You see the physical and emotional manifestations of pain avoidance everywhere.

I know from experience that food doesn't cancel the pain. I also know that you can buy all the shoes and backpacks in the world, and the pain still comes back. The distraction those substitutes offer is extremely temporary.

We might even try to substitute work for pain, thinking that being a workaholic will help. American culture celebrates being a hard worker, giving you an excuse for what you're doing. You're too busy to feel, think about, or deal with the pain. Heck, you're too busy to even remember what the pain is. But, like all the other substitutions and distractions, the pain is still there, working its way to the surface, and those temporary fixes only add to the terrible end result.

There are several ways to avoid pain, and at this point in the chapter, I've already used a couple of them in order to avoid getting to the point.

I'm ashamed of what I've done, and shame is one of the ways we avoid pain. Yes, I could probably help a lot of people with my story, but then I have to expose all of my garbage for everyone to see. I don't want people to know my secrets. I don't want to wonder what they're thinking about me. I don't want my daughters to think less of me as a man. And I definitely don't want to hurt my wife again by rehashing everything. Why do you think I started this chapter off with an amusing story? I want you to be predisposed to like me.

I'm about to tell you a secret, something really difficult to talk about, about what happened on one of the worst nights of my life. I'm about to let you behind the curtain to see an event that eventually kickstarted this book.

Diving Into the Pain

In August 2020, I was caught. Something that had started when I was a kid finally saw the light of day.

My dad was a pastor. I had a sheltered life as a kid. If we were going to do any reading in the house, it was going to be the Bible, the sports section, or my homework.

I had friends who had very different home lives, though. They had different reading material, and I use the term "reading" lightly because it was mostly about the pictures. They're referred to as "adult" magazines, but they're not good for anyone at any age. They were pornographic magazines, distorted and twisted versions of women and sex; and I learned to rely on them when pain and hurt became so unbearable that I needed that release. I found excuses to stay over at those friends' homes or do projects at their houses. My parents never knew.

I carried a lot of good things from my childhood into my adult years; but I also carried some bad things, including that addiction to pornography. Fighting this was a constant battle; but I was certain that when Tiffany and I got married, it wouldn't be a problem anymore. I figured the problem would go away.

It did, until it didn't.

If you've ever seen my wife, Tiffany, you're probably wondering how I could be so stupid. Tiffany is gorgeous. Believe me, I asked myself this all the time, and I was so ashamed that this was still destroying me. I had a living, breathing, amazing, beautiful wife; and I couldn't stop looking at pornography? I would go months away from it, sometimes even years, but then I would slip up. What kind of pastor, what kind of leader, what kind of Christian author would do such a thing?

So again, one August night back in 2020, I was watching a game on TV by myself, minding my own business, doing some armchair coaching. I paused the TV to get a snack, and when I came back, the screensaver mode was on. It was showing an advertisement for a free weekend trial of Showtime.

Immediately, I knew what that meant.

My heart started racing as childhood memories flooded me. I could almost feel fingers wrapping around my chest, making it hard to breathe.

What I should have done was what Joseph did when he ran from Potiphar's wife. I should have left the room, turned the TV off, screamed for help—anything but stay in that room.

I didn't.

I'll just check it out for a second, I thought as I sat down with the remote. *Maybe there's a good movie that I can't see on my current channels.*

I wasn't looking for a good movie. I knew exactly what I was looking for; and sure enough, I found it. I thought I was all alone, watching that garbage play out on the screen. Honestly, it hadn't even started yet, but that doesn't make me better or mean I haven't done this countless times before.

And then Tiffany walked in.

What I remember most was the sound of the slamming door as she left.

Pain substitutes crash and burn quickly, especially in moments like that; and I found myself going from enjoying the game and a snack to being in significant despair and shame, wondering if Tiffany was going to leave me for good. I turned the TV off but couldn't get any sleep that night.

For the next day or so, Tiffany wouldn't even talk to me. We pretended everything was fine around the girls, but I couldn't even get her to respond to a text. I didn't blame her because I knew I hurt her deeply again. When Monday morning rolled around, I was desperate to get some help and fix this problem that had been gnawing at me my whole life. I thought that if I showed her I was getting help, that I wanted to change and be held accountable, maybe she wouldn't leave me. It seemed as if I was on the verge of losing everything that mattered to me.

I texted six of my guy friends. I shared what had happened and told them that I needed accountability, that I needed help. Rusty, who was the husband part of our tag team marriage coaches, agreed to jump on a Zoom call and meet with me. We use them to invest in our marriage; but this time, I felt useless and helpless.

And then for some reason, Tiffany showed me incredible grace and love that same day.

I could see a change come over her, one that was almost tangible. She forgave me, and then she asked me to meet with Dave, who would become my life coach and an incredibly important man in my life.

"Andy, I'm not leaving you," she said. "I want you to go meet with Dave. You need to talk to him."

When you go meet a stranger who knows your dirty secrets, there's a fear and shame factor already at work on you when you walk in the door. Are they going to judge? Smirk? Talk down to you? Our culture today is so quick to judge and destroy—one mistake means you're canceled. I wasn't sure what to expect from a man I didn't even know.

Instead of judgment, Dave met me with grace and dignity. He showed me respect, even when I was primed to grovel in shame. Remember, shame is a kind of pain avoidance; living in shame and constant humiliation is a way to excuse sinful behavior. Being treated with respect when you don't think you deserve it cuts to the core.

Exposing my pain and fear to the light by telling my closest friends and letting them delve even deeper meant I gave less power to the darkness. We have this weird idea that our darkest secret sins and fears must never see the light, forgetting that we're only making the darkness more powerful when we do that. Light cleanses. And when we bring things out into the light, we gain clarity as we allow God, and the people He directs us to for help, to work. The more I talked about what was going on, the more understanding I had.

> *Being treated with respect when you don't think you deserve it cuts to the core.*

"I want to tell you about a dream I had," Dave told me during one of our conversations. He described how he'd dreamed he'd died, and that he was standing before God in Heaven. He was terrified that God was about ready to show him all of his faults and sins. Everyone would know! They'd see everything he'd done! But then something amazing happened.

Jesus was there, and He reached out and pulled him in. He held him, and instead of terror over everyone seeing how horrible he was, he felt pure agape love. He felt all the things he had done right in his life—the good and true things, not the dark and filthy things.

There are two phrases we have a hard time believing, both of them made only of three words.

"It is finished," Jesus said on the cross before He died.

"I love you," He tells us over and over in His Word.

You might think, "Jesus, I know you died for my sins, but they are really bad. And maybe, just maybe, they're too bad to be forgiven. I have to earn your forgiveness."

"I took care of it on the cross. It is finished."

"But Jesus, how can you possibly love someone like me, with all the horrible things in my heart and mind? Don't you know what I've done? Shouldn't I have to suffer and work harder to be worthy? Don't I deserve pain and misery?"

"I love you. You are My child."

The free gift of grace is hard for us to grasp, and I know this personally. I'm just a man. A sinner who's been saved by that grace not because I'm good, but because God is good.

After working with Dave, I've since learned that to really find hope and help when it comes to the ways we avoid pain, we have to deal with the pain itself and not the substitute. Too many people treat the addiction without treating the reason it exists, and it's easy to trade one addiction for another. Untreated pain does not go away. Being scared to know its source, or how deep it goes, won't make you well.

"Andy, tell me about your childhood," Dave asked early on.

I had a great childhood, and I told him so. The best parents. Great brothers I looked up to. I was sure my pain was from the situation with Payton and that I blamed myself for it.

Dave wasn't convinced that was the source. After all, the pornography struggle had started when I was young, long before Payton was in the picture.

"Could your pain be self-doubt?" he finally asked me.

My head exploded. Well ... yes! I never felt like I lived up to the greatness I was surrounded by; having a great childhood actually made me feel *worse* about all my failures to live up to the impossible standards I'd imagined.

My thought was that I had a great upbringing, so how could I have ended up such a failure? In my own mind, I was the black sheep, the failure of the family. And when the enemy hooked me early on with the shame that came from pornography, it set me up for a destructive pattern of living in self-doubt. It's like being a child prodigy heaped with greatness and possibility early on, used to accolades and admiration, only to struggle with self-worth when others catch up to his skill when he's older. It's the overachieving high school senior voted most likely to succeed living a typical life after graduation. I had a great origin story, but I fumbled it almost right away. I doubted I could be anything, or do anything, of value.

When you live in self-doubt that long, it becomes your crutch. It did for me. I was so used to its voice in my head that I let it be an excuse for underachieving, not trying, or setting myself up for failure.

I'll never lose weight because I've always been fat. I'll never defeat this pornography addiction because I've struggled since I was a kid. I'll never be bold or aggressive because my brothers already took care of that department.

When you doubt yourself, it's OK to live with the results of that doubt. You hate the despair and shame, but you're also comfortable there until one night the person you love the most in the world walks in on you in your weakest moment and you realize you could've lost everything.

One of the reasons writing this book was so difficult but also incredibly meaningful is that, word by word, chapter by chapter, I'm writing myself into confidence. Every session I have with Dave does the same. That's the trick with self-doubt: it tells you that you can't start until you're good enough. But when you see it for what it is, you realize you start where you're at and work your way forward. Races don't start at the finish line; they start at the beginning.

As I gain confidence in the calling God placed on my life, I no longer get lost trying to find my place in other people's callings. Tiffany has her own calling, and she does it beautifully. I support her, and she supports me.

Food, work, shopping, drugs, alcohol, and pornography: these are the pain avoidance methods of choice today. I'm familiar with too many of them, and maybe you are, too. We all have pain, and most of us don't want to meet it head-on. I want to encourage you to seek help, to bring light into the darkness in your life.

Dave repeatedly tells me that the only way we get better is by diving into the pain. James 1:2–3 tells us to count it as pure joy when we face trials because the testing of our faith produces perseverance. That's a confusing verse if you're still avoiding pain. It won't make sense until you realize the pain principle Dave has taught me. At this point, I would boldly say that I love pain. Pain makes me grow! Yeah, it hurts, especially early on; but afterward, when you dive into it? The results are amazing.

So, dive into your pain. Don't be afraid to get help. Find good people who will help you face it, not people who will help you substitute for it.

Then, bring that pain to light, so you actually start to heal.

You can't see the pit in front of you if you're still wandering around in the dark. Sometimes a pit is just an innocent ad on your streaming TV, and you'll tumble right in if it's too dark to see clearly. Darkness hides and distorts. I remember as a child, I was playing at a friend's house late at night. In the wee hours of the morning, we happened to notice a man sitting in a recliner across the room, and we were terrified. We couldn't move; we never left that spot the rest of the night. The next day, we saw that it was a football helmet sitting on top of a backpack, but in the dark, it looked like a body and glowing skull. Shining light on something changes everything.

And finally, be totally committed.

Never leave yourself an out. Never keep the door cracked so you can go back to the darkness. I am 100 percent committed to Tiffany, my family, my friends, and my Savior. I'm 100 percent committed to attacking self-doubt. I'm 100 percent committed to guarding my heart the right way and partnering with God each day as I do that.

I know you've probably gone through a lot of painful things, probably more than I ever did. Every human being experiences hardships, and we all have two options in front of us: hide from the pain, or take hold of God's hand and dive into it so we can break through and let the light in. When light enters the darkness, we open our eyes to what's really all around us.

While visiting Maui, Tiffany insisted on what I jokingly call the dreaded Road to Hana day. It's a famous drive with lots of scenery and spots to stop and take photos and do all kinds of things, but I was just not looking forward to it. We'd done it a few years earlier with a bigger group. It hadn't gone as planned, the experience wasn't exactly delightful, and some in the group still joke about it to this day. This time it was just our family, but I wasn't excited.

"God, I need you to partner with me today," I prayed. "You know I don't want to do this. Please don't let me ruin this for our family."

We stopped at Pa'ia for an espresso. Tiffany knew that would help me start the day on good footing. And then we began the long trip, one without cell phone service and lots of winding road.

We stopped at a fresh pineapple stand and got the girls some pineapple. They got to drink some coconut water and even watched as the stand's friendly owner shucked a coconut, giving them a taste of the coconut meat.

Each scenic view we stopped at seemed to get better. One stop is known as the Garden of Eden, with trails through brilliant floral gardens, the landscape, and gorgeous views out across the Pacific Ocean.

"Is this what Heaven will be like?" one of my daughters asked me.

"I don't know, but it's going to be amazing," I said.

We went to Wai'ānapanapa State Park next, and the black sand beach was a huge hit. While Tiffany stayed with the girls for a quick swim, I decided to do a

On the Road to Hana.

little hiking and take as many photos as I could. I discovered a cave you could walk through to get to the shoreline. I saw endless trees and plants, the richest green colors you'll ever see. Rugged cliffs and soft-looking waterfalls seemed to be everywhere. At every turn, the ocean was like a sparkling blue jewel laid out forever. I struggled to put words to all of what I saw, talking to God in awe the whole time and feeling overwhelmed with a sense of peace and joy.

How did we miss this before? I wondered. *How could I have ever dreaded this day?*

The first time we did the Road to Hana, we'd been in a rush and had skipped the highlights to get to the hike at the end. This time was different. I had almost missed out.

Diving into pain isn't just about finishing the trip, getting to the end as quickly as possible. It's about the journey. What if I never wrote this book? What if that horrible night in August had never happened? What if I was still captive to self-doubt and trying to numb the pain?

God provides peace along the journey, and when you take the leap and confront pain with Him beside you, it won't be long before you wonder why you'd waited so long.

CHAPTER 9

Beauty in the Storm

The year 1984 was amazing. There's a reason why nostalgia for the eighties seems to drop right in that zone.

Van Halen's "Jump" and Kenny Loggins's "Footloose" were filling the airwaves. Lionel Richie was telling everyone "Hello." The Summer Olympics were held in Los Angeles, where Mary Lou Retton and Carl Lewis became household names. Doug Flutie took home the Heisman while at Boston College, and Larry Bird and the Celtics defeated Magic Johnson and the Lakers in an epic seven-game NBA finals.

And even more importantly, a wee lad named Anthony Blake Howard entered school for the first time, setting foot in kindergarten in Waco, Texas.

Take a moment and absorb this, both the crowning glory of the year and the fact that yes, my full name is Anthony but I go by Andy.

No, not Andrew. No, don't call me Tony. Call me Andy. If that's confusing, ask my mom. She has the goods on that one.

I remember that year of kindergarten so well, and one particular day stands out. A storm seemed to pop up out of nowhere. In Texas, everything is bigger, and that includes the weather surprises. The school building had a long stretch of rooms with doors that opened to the outside, sort of like a motel. If you're from the north lands where it gets cold, your school was probably different. That day of kindergarten was pretty typical. Blocks, nap, snack, Kleenexes, and then suddenly . . . the darkest, scariest sky I can remember. That part was atypical. It was the middle of the day and it felt like night; that was how dark it was.

I imagine it wasn't fun to be the teacher that day. I remember being told to play while I watched the teachers from the classrooms huddle up and talk about what was apparently the end of the world barrelling down the horizon. I could tell something was wrong. It was one thing to see a dark sky in the middle of the day, but another to see adults nervous and scared. Little kids look to adults for courage.

The teachers' huddle broke. "Come on kids, hurry hurry!" they said, leading us to a restroom and telling us to sit cross-legged on the floor.

By then, the rolling black clouds were fully on us, and with it came a roaring, howling wind. Some tucked their heads down, and others quietly sobbed. While I was shaken up a bit, I decided what the moment could really use was a stand-up comic. I wanted everyone to laugh with me instead of at me; and if I let myself get scared, I definitely could have seen the latter happen.

So there, sitting on the floor of the restroom with crying kids and a screaming wind, I pulled out my schoolwork.

"I'm not scared," I said, terrified.

As the rain and hail slammed the ground, a tornado went through the Waco area. Yet my four-year-old street cred was unharmed. I don't know how long this storm went on before it waned, but I do remember the moment my teacher spoke up.

"Andy, your dad is here," she said.

I grabbed my stuff and ran to him as fast as I could; and when I reached him, I broke down crying. I was scared the whole time, and when my dad walked into the room, I could safely let my guard down because he knew me. No need to front. I always felt safe with my dad. He was there to walk me home, and everything would be OK.

Wouldn't it be nice if we didn't have those scary storms? Couldn't we have nice sunny days without the terror? If nothing else, at least pea-sized hail instead of icy baseballs hurled at our foreheads from angry clouds would be nice.

Think of the earth, a giant ball of mud and flowers and farms and pollution and animals and lakes and concrete-infused cities— everything that exists on the planet. As terrifying as that storm was for me and the thousands of others who were affected, it was necessary.

Without thunderstorms, we'd be in a real mess.[9] Those storms bring moisture and spread seeds and pollen, and the wind and updrafts help scour out pollution from the ground level, taking it up high and away. If there were no thunderstorms, there'd be a lot more deserts or arid regions. We'd have Sahara 1, 2, and 3.

Think of that other terrifying pulverizer from the sky: the hurricane. In the same way, hurricanes are more than just destructive; they help us out. They bring much-needed moisture, but they also break up bacteria or a red tide by oxygenating the ocean water. Like other storms, they balance the heat between the poles and the equator, keeping us from extremes as they spread seeds and potential plant life far from where they'd normally fall.[10]

Max Lucado tells a story of a time when he and his wife bought a boat. He was new to owning a boat, and a hurricane was coming through. He knew that if he didn't anchor his boat he would lose it, so he went out to try to figure out how to tie it down. He tied it to the deck. He tied it to a tree. He tied it to whatever he could think of.

A former marine walked by and saw what he was doing. "That's not going to work," he told Lucado. "When a storm like this comes through, you have to anchor deep."

You have to anchor deep.

No one likes going through a storm. They're scary and dangerous. You might end up with damaged property. You might end up sitting on the floor next to the toilet trying to do some schoolwork or hiding in a bathtub as the roof above you blows away. But you know what?

When we go through a storm, we have the ability to help others the next time, even if it's as basic as showing them that storms are survivable. After I made it through that storm at the school with my father, holding his hand as we walked home, I felt more confident the next time there was a storm. We aren't promised a storm-free life, but we are promised to never

9   Heba Soffar, "Thunderstorms advantages, disadvantages, effects & types," *Online Sciences*, last modified March 12, 2021, https://www.online-sciences.com/the-environment/thunderstorms-advantages-and-disadvantages/.

10   Jonathan Belles, "5 Things Hurricanes Can Do That Are Actually Good," *The Weather Channel*, last modified August 29, 2017, https://weather.com/storms/hurricane/news/hurricane-landfall-benefits-2016.

walk through it alone. If we anchor deep with God, no matter how hard the winds, we can trust His hand on our life and walk through the storm.

That's hard to remember in the midst of the storm, though. Even the disciples, who walked with Jesus and had Him on their actual boat, forgot. In Mark 4:35–41, we read about a terrifying storm that almost swamped the disciples' boats, all while Jesus was taking a nap. When He calmed the waters, the disciples—even after listening to Him teach and seeing His miracles—were still surprised.

"Why are you so afraid?" He asked them. "Do you still have no faith?"

Tiffany and I have learned firsthand that storms are scary, not just because of the winds and damage, but because of how they challenge us to exercise our faith. When we doubt God, we are more afraid of what He might lead us through, and we take our eyes off our Father and put them on the wind and the waves instead.

More Bills Than Bank Account

I was jolted awake with a screeching sound. In a mental fog, I wasn't sure if it was an alarm. I quickly realized it was someone screaming, a bone-breaking and horrible sound I'd never heard before.

Tiffany. Tiffany was screaming.

I jumped out of bed, completely confused, my heart racing and my body shifting into battle mode. *Get up. Find your wife.*

"Tiffany!" I hollered as I staggered toward the door. I could still hear her screaming. I feared the worst.

A few years earlier, Tiffany's dad, Gary, had passed away from cancer; and her mom, Jeannie, was really struggling. Jeannie never really got over the loss. Tiffany missed her dad, too, but losing a spouse is different. Your partner in life, the one you relied on, the one in all your memories, the one smiling next to you in every vacation photo album, the one you built your family with. The whole life she'd built with her husband was taken from her. Gone, like a piece of flesh ripped out. We could see how it affected her, even though I couldn't imagine what she must have felt.

She found herself alone in a big house with a lot of land, and she was miserable. Everywhere she looked was a reminder of Gary. It was heartbreaking to watch her struggle through this loneliness, and we decided

We aren't promised a storm-free life, but we are promised to never walk through it alone.

to move closer to her. We found a house halfway between where we were living and where she lived, but our finances were such a mess that we didn't have the credit to buy it.

Jeannie had great credit, though, and she wanted a fresh start. It seemed as if everything came together. We decided together that she'd move in with us, we'd help her, and she could help us. We made the payments; she supplied the credit.

Tiffany and her mom Jeannie on our wedding day.

It was a good year with Tiffany's mom living with us. We all quickly adapted and formed habits around each other's life rhythms. We helped her through her grief, and her wisdom and love helped us through the struggles we were dealing with. She would also help us with some expenses, and it seemed like we were in a good place.

But now, there was terrifying screaming. Angry wind was blowing again.

"Help!" Tiffany was screaming. "Help! Please God, no! Help! She's gone, she's dead!"

I was sure something had happened to baby Payton. Tiffany always got up early to start Payton's early morning routines; and as I rushed to where the screaming was coming from, I tried to prepare myself for what I would find.

I found Tiffany standing over her mother's body.

Jeannie had been getting ready for work that morning, a typical start to the day, but at some point had had a massive heart attack. She wasn't overweight. She wasn't unhealthy. Nothing indicated she was in danger.

What she died from is something called broken heart syndrome.

She'd mourned herself to death.

Losing Jeannie so unexpectedly was devastating. She had always been important to us; but it also felt like the new, beautiful chapter of life we had just started with her was deleted. We spent the last year becoming a strong family unit. Things clicked. Our struggles didn't seem as overwhelming with Jeannie's knowledge and unending love filling our home. But that was all gone now.

To say it was a monumental loss is an understatement. Especially considering the many losses our family had already suffered. By age twenty-five, Tiffany had lost her sister, her dad, and now her mother. My own father was struggling with cancer.

We were plummeting into dark days.

Not only were we grieving Jeannie's shocking passing, but our home life and financial situation had suddenly changed, too. While Tiffany's mom wasn't rich, she managed money well. She'd given us sound advice and even helped us when we needed it most—whether it was one of Payton's medical bills or any of the financial hurdles that always loomed. Now our safety net, both financially and emotionally, was ripped to shreds.

We barely had time to deal with our grief before the bills started piling up. I'm not talking about your typical bills, either. I'm talking about the bills stamped with bold red letters. The ones that shouted: "You're in serious trouble!" I wasn't getting any letters from Jesus, just debt collectors; and they have a significantly different tone.

We tried. We tried to pay our bills, but there were so many of them. I was working as a youth minister at the time, a part-time position with full-time demand, which is typical with ministry. I worked full-time as an order filler on the weekends for a large corporation's distribution center. During the week I also worked full-time as a data entry clerk, and I even picked up additional income helping with the church landscaping, work that was much more arduous and time-consuming than I was aware it would be when I agreed to do it. It was Texas, after all, and triple-digit hot. By the time I was done with the work, 10 hours had gone by. I was forever grateful for the opportunity to earn money, though. Tiffany helped with some administrative tasks as well as helping clean the church, and that would take her many hours, too. The Lord was faithful in giving us opportunities, and as we worked hard, He provided. Every cent counted.

But we knew it was just a matter of time before the levee broke. We were holding our financial burdens back with prayer, duct tape, and chicken wire. Each day, we were scratching out survival, and it was hard on the family. Anyone who's been there, who's lived in the land of low income and high bills, knows you get good at juggling. You pay one bill one month, and the next bill another month. You juggle payments and missed payments to keep under the radar, but you never fully catch up. It's not a good thing to do, but we owed more than we made; so it was impossible to balance out the columns.

With Jeannie's passing, not only were we now paying the entire note on the house, but we inherited her new car. We loved that car. It had become Tiffany's safe place, where her mother's presence was almost tangible, from the smell to the little handwritten notes Jeannie had left behind. We loved it, but we also knew we couldn't afford it. The car payments sat there, another bill on the stack that was crushing us.

The burden and darkness of the time was so thick and heavy. Payton's health challenges came with bills that were at an all-time high. Tiffany slipped into depression. My dad was getting sicker each day from cancer.

One night, as I was sitting at home trying to both figure out what to pay and how to cope, someone started pounding on the front door. This was not the pleasant knocking of a salesman or someone handing out religious literature. This was loud and insistent.

I opened a door, and there they were, my first experience with repo men.

"We're here to take the car."

My face grew hot. There was nothing I could do. I didn't have a cent on me. If I'd known it was them, I probably wouldn't have answered the door because that was an experience I could have done without. They could've just taken the car from the driveway without us having to feel humiliated in the doorway.

"Please—is there anything I can do to keep it?" I asked.

The man handed me a contact card and said I could call the number if I wanted to catch up on payments, but right now they had to take the vehicle. He was nice about it, and I understood he was just doing his job, but this was yet another awful moment.

"Don't let them take it! Don't let them take it!" Tiffany said, running up behind me as I stood in the doorway. This was her mom's car, the one place Tiffany would go to feel her presence.

The man turned and left. Tiffany tried to go outside, but I grabbed her. She beat her fist into my chest.

"Please don't let them take it!" she wailed. "How can you do this?"

I have rarely felt less like a man than I did at that moment. I felt like a complete and total failure, and it's definitely on my list of worst moments in my life. I felt helpless and alone, and I had to watch my wife's heart shatter as her mom's car was taken away.

Life in the financial blackhole is a grind. There's a constant undercurrent of fear and stress, and every moment of existence is like an accounting ledger. What will this cost? What can we afford to do? What will we pay? What will we do without? You can't enjoy anything without thinking about the price tag.

Many times, we were hours away from having our electricity shut off. I'd have to swallow my pride—when you don't have enough money to pay your bills, pride gets in the way—and ask for help from friends. Some weeks they'd help us, and we'd try to help them back when it was their turn in need. Yet asking for help is difficult for a man. (Just one notch above asking for directions.) Every time I asked for help, it was a reminder that I couldn't provide for my family. A man was supposed to provide for his family, and I wasn't doing the most basic thing required of me.

Frankly, I don't know how we stayed afloat. I don't know how we didn't capsize in that storm. It's all a dark blur.

We adopted a triage mentality where bills were categorized by what must be paid all the way down to what we could put off paying. The house always came first, though we never seemed to catch up on those payments, either. We were always living on the last-month warning, making the monthly payment many months late. In other words, the bill we paid wasn't a mortgage bill: it was an eviction notice. More often than I'd like to admit, we found ourselves down to the last day or two, sometimes calling and begging for extensions. We had to have a home.

We started selling off whatever we could to make money. Tiffany's mom had purchased a new John Deere riding lawn mower for $2,000 when she moved in. It was about the only thing left that had real value, but no one wanted to pay what it was worth. Finally, we had one man interested in meeting me at the house so he could see the mower. He was offering $700.

That was far too low, but I was desperate. The whole day at work, I watched the clock. I couldn't miss meeting that guy because that was going to be our house payment that month. Then, I got a text from my pastor wanting to have a meeting. I kind of hoped it was going to be some kind of "look at this miracle that God did to provide for you" meeting that ended with a check in an envelope, but it was a routine meeting about how things were going in the youth department. As the clock on the wall ticked by, and it was clear I was going to be late for the lawn mower appointment, I imagined I'd just lost the house.

If I'd have told the pastor what was going on in our lives, I have no doubt he would've helped us or come up with a way to figure something out. But I had too much pride and didn't want to ask for help. In fact, during that meeting when he asked how we were doing, I told him we were doing great instead of telling him I'd decided to rest the safety and security of my family on the sale of a lawn mower. When the meeting was over, I roared out of the parking lot. The potential buyer agreed to stick around when I told him I'd be late.

The buyer knew he had me in a tight spot. He could smell the desperation all over me. After giving the like-new lawn mower a once-over, he said the best he could do was $600. He was getting a steal from a desperate man, and he knew it. He had the leverage; I didn't.

I was sick to my stomach selling it at such a low price, but that $600 bought us thirty more days in the house. Thirty more days with a roof over our head. Thirty more days to fight the unwinnable fight.

If I wanted to write a book of stories like this, stories that come from being broke and in debt, I could. There were many, and they all had lots of gory, soul-crushing details.

But that's not the point.

The takeaway from all of this is to show that this was an extended period of our lives where we were emotionally, physically, and financially exhausted. It was a miracle of God that we survived. We like to think God's miracles are checks that arrive in the mail that cover all the bills (and yes, something like that happened to us); but sometimes, as He leads us through the refining fire, they are miracles of just-enough daily-bread provision that cause us to rely on Him all the more. His timing is not our timing, and while He might ask you to give up your lawn mower now, He knows what He has planned for you down the road.

> *It was a miracle of God
> that we survived.*

On New Year's Eve of 2015, my mom called me.

"Honey," she said. "I was watching a preacher on TV. He asked for anyone who needed a financial miracle to sow a seed into their ministry."

I don't recommend people send money to just anyone you see on TV, but my mom has always been very in tune with the Lord. If He asks her to do something, she's faithful and obeys.

"I sent $20 for myself, and $20 for your family."

I thanked her, but I didn't really know what to think. TV preacher? Really?

Little did I know, something better was coming.

A Thread of Faithfulness

Talking about the hard times is easier than talking about the good times.

Misery loves company, and everyone hangs on the drama that naturally comes out of hard times. Did they make it through? What did they lose? Who cried? What happened next? Could it get any worse?

It's easier to hold an audience when they're hanging onto every detail of the story of your terrible, no good, very bad day. But there's an added dimension for me, and it's questioning why God has been so good to us. Our life right now is crazy good, and I can't understand it. Why us? Do we deserve this life?

No, we don't.

My Mom was visiting us at a recent Thanksgiving and saw our house for the first time. As she looked around, I knew she was remembering all we'd gone through. Tears filled her eyes, and she began to weep softly. She grabbed my arm.

"Andy, God has blessed you because you never lost the faith," she said. "You've remained faithful through it all."

Me and my momma! I'm forever grateful to be her son.

Mom is always right, but I still have a hard time believing it because God has been so, so good. I don't know how to share the details about the good times without running full speed into the wall of embarrassment because I was always taught to be humble. If you know my personality, you know I'm getting a little red-faced just writing this.

But here's the thing: what I'm about to share isn't about me. It's not about how good I am and how I deserve good things. What I'm about to share is an attempt to show you just how good God is by showing you how far He brought us from the days of juggling bills, repo men, and hoping a TV preacher wasn't lying.

As kids, our home was filled with love. But there were five boys, and Mom and Dad didn't have a lot of money. Each Christmas, there was a husband and wife in the church who would play Santa, and after everyone had left the Sunday night service right before Christmas, they would give my brothers and I some gifts. Having kids of my own, I know that must've melted my parents' hearts, that someone in the church would show such kindness to their boys. Another family, who had kids about the same age as us, would bring trash bags full of clothes they were getting rid of, and we were so excited to get some "new" clothes. Sometimes, people would give my dad the infamous "$100 handshake" and slip him some extra cash because the Lord had directed them to meet our unspoken need.

Today, Tiffany and I get to play Santa.

We are able to help other families in need and provide opportunities for busy moms to work from home and be there for their families. We help kids go to summer camp because I know how important that is and how it hurts when you miss out. We've provided employment opportunities for people who need jobs, and they work right at our house, helping with Payton. I was thrilled that we were able to help move my mom, who has some of her own health struggles now, into assisted living. We support many missionaries and churches each month, trying to be obedient to the Lord's leading. We've given away an expensive minivan that's been custom fit for a child with special needs and a wheelchair, complete with a lift. For years, we wanted one for Payton but had to struggle with setting her wheelchair up and breaking it down in the Texas heat every time we went to the doctor. Or we'd get wet when it rained. Just the wear and tear of transferring her from the special needs car seat to her wheelchair was hard on all of us. I know what it's like to need that van, and we knew God had someone in mind for it.

We went from nearly homeless if not for the sale of a lawn mower to being able to do this. From a bank account in the red and the bills to match to financial plenty. From selling everything we could to hiring people to work for us. And it was all God. God's provision, God's grace, God's generosity. We simply obey and give generously as He directs. He is always leading people into our path.

One afternoon, while waiting at the dealership to get the oil changed in my car, I overheard the service man tell a woman that her vehicle was going to need significantly more expensive repair than they'd previously thought.

"It's going to cost an extra $600," he told her.

Her face paled, and I could see she was worried.

I knew what she was feeling; she was mentally calculating how she was going to juggle that month's bills in light of this surprise expense. I walked over to the man, who was now at the counter.

"I want to cover her bill," I said. I didn't even have to check with Tiffany. God was very clear that He wanted me to do this, and she'd support this 100 percent.

It is a joy and a privilege when God helps you to a place where you can exercise generosity. We serve a generous God, and He allows us to mimic Him. Having lived through the times of playing Russian roulette at the grocery store cash register, where you hope and pray your card goes through, and experience the embarrassment when it doesn't and they have to call the bank—it's a lot of fun to buy other people's groceries when God leads me to do so.

Please, please, please understand this isn't so I get a pat on the back.

I'm not trying to impress you with my success because it isn't just mine. While we were always willing to work hard and obey God, I can't take all of the credit. I don't know how else to illustrate the incredible faithfulness of a generous and giving God than to illustrate the journey from not being able to pay our own bills to eventually being able to help pay others' bills. That same illustration helps me keep a right perspective.

It reminds me yet again how much beauty there is in the broken, and it gives me a thankful heart, one that is grateful to God for every single good thing we have today. Knowing the pain of being in need makes the joy of giving all that much more wonderful. The journey is never, ever wasted, no matter how scary it is.

I often think of God calling Abraham and asking him to leave everything and everyone he knew so He could lead him someplace completely different. I imagine it went something like this:

"Where am I going?" Abraham asked, after God told him to pack up his household and hit the camel trail.

"You leave that up to me. Just go where I lead you."

"But the journey would be so much less stressful if I knew where I was going to end up."

"You will have to trust me."

"So no hints, then."

"I will lead you through."

Trust is never easy, but it's made easier when you know the one doing the leading is good and generous and full of grace and completely trustworthy. Walking outside after that big Waco storm was possible because I fully trusted my dad.

We discover more about the nature of God, and who God is, when we trust Him in the difficult journey. We get to experience His provision along the way. The more we trust God, the more we learn we can *continue* to trust God with increasing confidence. You might not have all the details of where you're going, and you might not have the same amount of faith and trust in the beginning as you will have at the end, but you can still take the first step in obedience.

Remember that six-week youth pastor nightmare I told you about earlier? When I got back to Texas, feeling a bit like a failure and completely lost in life, I only had about $20 to my name. We'd followed God's lead to Florida, and now we were back again. We knew of a nearby church that had been looking for a youth pastor. I spent our last $20 taking the pastor to lunch to hopefully talk about the open youth pastor position. At that lunch, he told me they'd just hired one. It seemed like God was leading us into closed doors. Yet the same evening that I learned the youth pastor job wasn't available, my cousin called and said they had some job openings for the company she worked for. My Father is always faithful.

> *The more we trust God, the more we learn we can* continue *to trust God with increasing confidence.*

Our family during our Make-A-Wish trip. We are so blessed to be able to help others now!

Partnering With Our Father

While working with my coach, Dave, I had one of those moments where you see something new in a passage of Scripture even though you've read it a hundred times before. We were having a conversation about the book of Exodus, specifically the "I Am" passage.[11]

There's Moses, in front of the burning bush that won't burn, God speaking to him and telling him He wants old Moses to go to Egypt and lead the Israelites out of slavery.

Moses had lots of concerns about that, one of which was what he would say.

"Suppose I go to the Israelites and tell them 'The God of your fathers has sent me to you,' and they ask me 'What is His name?'" Moses said. "What should I tell them?"

"I AM WHO I AM," God replied. "This is what you are to say to the Israelites. Tell them 'I AM has sent me to you.'"

I AM. That's pretty awesome.

11   *Exodus 3:13–14.*

We fill our social media profiles with every impressive thing we can, fill our feeds with selfies and images meant to show everyone how amazing we are. We use lots of words and photos to try to explain who we are. But you ask God who He is, and all He has to say is I AM. In just two words, He speaks the truth about who He is.

I've heard it said that the best liar speaks mostly truth, but they just bend it a little bit. They use plenty of words and tuck a few lies in them somewhere, like putting a tiny bit of poison in the sugar. It tastes pretty sweet until suddenly you can't taste anymore because you're toe-up on the floor. Mostly-truth is tough. The great preacher Charles Spurgeon said that "discernment is not knowing the difference between right and wrong. It is knowing the difference between right and almost right."

The devil is very good at deceiving. In John 8:44, we're told he was a murderer from the beginning and that there's no truth in him because his native language is lying. He's the father of lies.

"That's great, Andy," you're probably thinking, "but what does that have to do with Moses at the burning bush?"

For over a decade, I didn't write this book because I listened to the father of lies. I had a list of I AM NOT that told me why I shouldn't start. I am not qualified. I am not a writer. I am not an influencer. I am not smart enough. I am not (fill in the blank). The list was endless. But Dave told me to partner with God when I wrote this book; in other words, instead of relying on the I AM NOT, I would put my trust in the great I AM.

One of the tools Dave gave me that we still use daily is "the hatchet." It's not a real hatchet—let's not get crazy here. It's a metaphorical hatchet, like those foam versions you'd see at an Atlanta Braves or Kansas City Chiefs game. You literally just make the motion with your own hand.

"Every time you find yourself saying 'I am not,' I want you to chop off the 'not,'" he told me. "Do it at that moment. Right there. Don't give it power by letting it sit."

Admittedly, it can feel a little silly at times, and some days, I feel like I spend an awful lot of time "chopping." But what it does is make me aware of how often I add the "not" to my thoughts.

I am because I've partnered with the I AM.

When I'm weak and struggling, I'm glad I get my identity from the great I AM. For too many years, I struggled with identity, trying to create an image (the kindergarten comedian in the bathroom, for example) or relying on my job to define me. It's exhausting and fearful to get your identity from things that change, whether it's a pink slip or cultural trends telling you how to define yourself. You're constantly on stage performing the identity, making sure it plays true to character.

When I finally grasped what it was like to partner with my Heavenly Father, it was just like that day at school. I could be real, and I could walk home through the storm with my father, tears and all. I am not what I do. I am because of I AM. I am His creation. I am loved by Him. Nothing I do (or do not do) will make Him love me any less. It's a process, getting comfortable with I AM, but it's worth it. I went from telling people that I was *trying* to write a book to telling them that I *was* writing a book.

The lying, deceiving devil does a great job with identity theft, though, and there are too many people who have fallen for I AM NOT.

When I first met my father-in-law, I was terrified of him. Gary was an amazing man, but he scared me to death. One evening, Tiffany, her parents, and I went out to eat dinner together. I probably only got two bites down, and you know I love to eat. That's the fear level we're talking about here.

At that time, Gary wasn't attending church anymore. I never asked what happened, but it bothered Tiffany's mom. She'd get upset when he wouldn't come with her to church, but there was no budging him.

Not long after Tiffany and I started dating, her sister Kim died.

That was a huge, heavy storm.

When a storm arrives, it's OK to ask God why. He's a big God, and He can take it. The Bible tells us He weeps, too. Not because He's surprised or powerless, but because He hates to see us hurt, even though He knows good will come from storms.

When He tells us in Matthew 11:28–30 that His yoke is easy and His burden is light, He means it. A yoke is a wooden crossbeam that connects two animals, making it possible for them to work together in the same direction. Did you know you can't partner with someone without a yoke? Each day when I wake up, I ask God to help me partner with Him. How will we write this book? How can we serve someone?

He never intended for you to carry the burdens and hurts that come with those storms all alone. He put the weight of the world on his son

Jesus, who died on those wooden beams that made up the cross and paid for all of it.

But the storms still come, and Tiffany's sister died, and we were all heartbroken. It seemed like there could be nothing good from such a loss, from so much pain. A lot of people, when they find themselves in a storm, shake their fist at God instead of running to Him to walk through it with Him. Instead of partnering with Him, they divorce themselves from Him.

Gary was like me, that kindergartner sitting on the bathroom floor. In the midst of the storm, he didn't turn from God, even though he lost his daughter.

"Gary, your Father is here."

He ran to God, tears and all.

What very easily could have sent him over the edge sent him right to God instead, and I can't tell you what it was like to see the family come together again, spiritually whole. Down the road, he even became a deacon at the church and active in men's ministry.

Because of the storm, he found his identity in I AM.

All Things Made New

One of the weird things that happens with storms is that you can smell them.

You know what I'm talking about. It's that smell we associate with rain. It's actually part of the reaction of the lightning with the air, when it splits the oxygen and nitrogen atoms and creates ozone. It's a clean smell that comes with the rest of the storm. Something in the air has changed. The same is true of storms in our lives: they change us.

Maybe you hear the story about Gary and don't feel encouraged. "That's great for Gary, but I've wasted too much time at this point," you might be thinking. "I ran the other way for so long, I'll never get back. I can't even remember who I was."

Maybe. But just like Dave gave me the hatchet, let me give you one of mine. I call it the "so what." (OK, so I haven't come up with an ingenious name. I'm working on it.)

You tell me all of that, and I would say, "So what?"

If you have today and right now, you can partner with the I AM. You can start new, right now. You don't have to go back down some road you got lost on and make up for past time. Your current location in the timeline of your life is the best starting point you'll ever have. You'll never find a starting point in the past.

Let's say you were told today was your last day to live.

"Hey, buddy, at 10 p.m. tonight, it's go time," God says to you. Exciting news, indeed.

Wouldn't those last few hours carry more weight than any hour ever before? Believe me, I'm absolutely excited to get to Heaven because it's beyond words or imagination—pure gold streets, for crying out loud—but our life down here is a gift with meaning, too.

Are you going to spend those last hours thinking it's too late to make up for lost time, or will you take the time you have left and partner with God? Are you going to think of all the storms that created brokenness, or take a gulp of fresh, new air? You would cherish every waking moment instead of thinking about the past moments that you can't do anything about, I hope.

Brewster's Millions was a movie from the 1980s where a man had to spend $30 million in thirty days if he wanted to inherit the remaining $300 million. There were all kinds of tricky stipulations and things didn't go well because, as it turns out, it's hard to spend that much money that fast. But let's shave that down a bit, and I'll translate it into an illustration I used when I was a youth pastor. I'd tell the kids to imagine I gave them $1,440, but they had to spend it all by midnight. Everything that was unused was taken away at midnight. Would they still take the money?

Yes. All of the youth would tell me yes, and they'd tell me about the iPhones and shoes and clothes and cars—

"You guys, it's only $1,440," I'd remind them. Perspective.

I'd then say, "What if I gave you $10,080? The catch is, you have to spend it in a week, and everything unused at the end of the week is lost. Deal?"

Absolutely. They thought that would be amazing!

"What if I gave you $525,600? You have a year to spend it. Everything unused will be lost at the end."

Heck yes, they'd take that deal. By now, they were usually pretty excited and planning elaborate vacations and extravagant purchases. That was the moment to bring them back to reality.

"There are 1,440 minutes in each day, 10,080 minutes in each week, and 525,600 minutes in a year. How will you spend them?" They got quiet as they thought about what I was saying.

If this was your last day, you'd cherish each hour. The Bible tells us that no one knows how long they have to live, and that we don't know what day is our last day. We have to make the most of each one; there are no more excuses about the minutes you've already spent.

When I started jotting down ideas for this book, it was the start of 2020. That sounded like it should have been a cool year, right? A brand-new beginning with the excitement of a new decade, plus the cool number 2020. Should be golden, right? I love the idea of a new year because it's a chance to reflect and refocus, a chance to check the inventory on what went well or not-so-well the previous year. In truth, though, our January 1 vision of the year is always very different from the view we have on December 31.

> *If this was your last day, you'd cherish each hour.*

Similarly, what we imagined on January 1, 2020 was not at all how the year went. Yet even in the chaos of 2020, God blessed our family. We stayed healthy, and our business grew despite the hardships that were going on. And when 2021 rolled around, we did the same thing we always do: we asked ourselves what went well and what we needed to change. No minute, no hour, and no day is wasted, no matter if Hurricane 2020 blew through. It's all a chance to grow, to start fresh.

One year, my brother and I were playing *Tecmo Bowl*. If you don't know what that is, I sadly place you in the category of people who missed out on a truly amazing Nintendo football game. Kids today don't know how hard we had it back then, our chunky pixelated graphics so much different from today's incredible gaming systems. Tough times.

Anyway, my brother had Bo Jackson as his player, which was, if you were honest, a built-in cheat code. Who could stop Bo Jackson? If you had him, you could run around the entire football field if you wanted and run the clock down for the quarter, scoring at the last moment.

My competitive nature had a problem with this. Sometimes, I'd wait for just the perfect moment to hit the reset button on the Nintendo and crush my brother's digital hopes and dreams. This usually led to a burst of anger and me getting punched (with great amounts of brotherly love, I'm sure), but it was the only way I could figure out how to not lose to Bo Jackson.

If you're not happy with your life, you have two options: do what you've always done, or hit reset.

Too many pick the first option, complaining or finding themselves lost in a life they don't like, yet unwilling to do anything differently. Perhaps the storms of life—storms they have tried to go through alone—have beat them down to the point where they don't think they have the energy to try again. So, they do what they always do, crushed and weary, wanting change but unwilling to change anything.

Maybe you've heard of that famous phrase that insanity is doing the same thing over and over again and expecting different results. Imagine you changed just one or two small things and the effect that would have. Maybe you stop going grocery shopping when you're hungry, or you start parking your car at the end of the parking lot to get in more walking. Maybe you limit your TV time so you sleep better and can get up earlier to read the Bible before heading off to work. Every year comes with 12 chapters and 365 blank pages, and you get a chance to write something new every single day.

Think of the potential of those blank pages. And think of the faithfulness of the One who helps us write them.

Hebrews 12:2 tells us that Jesus is the author and finisher of our faith, and in Philippians 1:6, we learn that He is the one who started that good work in you and that He will carry it to completion. You can fight against God, or you can partner with Him; He is faithful and willing to help you write out the rest of your days, starting right now.

All of this—whether we're talking about the storms of life or how we can partner with God to get through them—is about faithfulness. There is beauty in the storm *because of faithfulness*.

Tiffany and I, holding on to our faith in the Lord, even when things seemed impossible yet again, giving to God whenever He told us to give. Mom, being faithful in what seemed like an odd thing, sending $40 to a TV preacher. Gary, putting his faith back in God in the midst of the storm, finding his true identity. God, showing us how faithful He is each time He got us through another day so that we could experience His good and faithful nature and trust where He led us.

My hope for you is that you realize you can put your trust in a faithful God.

God has you. He knows where He's leading you. He won't let your boat sink. He won't let you drown. He knows what's happening. He'll get you through.

When it seems like He doesn't hear your prayers, you wonder if He's forgotten you, the bill collectors are pounding at your door, and there are no other options that you can see . . . know that *He sees you*. He has not forgotten you. He loves and adores you. Those dark periods of life aren't times of abandonment but times where your trust and faith can grow the most, if you'll let it.

CHAPTER 10

Fabulously Flawed

By now, you probably know that I love sports. Playing sports, watching sports, suggesting to the athletes and coaches on TV how they could improve their game—the usual. I grew up so saturated in sports that it just seemed normal to me that everyone would love sports.

Imagine my surprise (and shock and horror) when I discovered that there were people who not only didn't share this same passion, but couldn't even identify any particulars other than "sportsball." Who knew there were so many folks out there with zero interest in sports? All potential friends of mine must be able to talk sports (I'm kidding). But I do have a lot of sports-infused friends.

Recently, my friend Todd blessed my sports-loving socks off. While I can't go into too much detail about who Todd is, he's a big deal. He'd be so embarrassed that I even said that, but here's a hint: his direct report is Stephen Jones.

Yes, Stephen Jones of the Dallas Cowboys. (For those of you who do not love sports, that is a football team of great significance, a team that I and others who know what they're talking about call "America's Team." Don't at me, bro.)

Anyway, Todd gave me a chance to watch my two favorite teams—the Cowboys and Texas A&M—all within eight days. We were given a suite and field passes, and I felt like I could reach out and touch Heaven. Add those two days to my short list of the greatest days of my life because there, just a few yards away, were my favorite players. My friend Adam even caught a pass from Dak Prescott! (If sportsball isn't your thing, try to work with me here.)

Me, Adam, Michael, and Mat before the Cowboys game.

We were walking and getting access to parts of the stadium that normal people don't get to stroll around in. Security kept stopping us, of course, because we didn't seem to belong. So, I'd say I was with Todd, they'd give us a look that said they'd need more than that to keep them from booting us out, and then Todd would walk up.

"They're with me," he'd say, and security would smile and get out of the way, waving us through with a welcome.

Wow. Everything was rolling along perfectly, and it felt like I owned the world (or at least the stadium). Todd was with us, and I could be confident in my swagger. At one point, Skip Pete, the running backs coach for the Cowboys, walked by.

"What's up?" I yelled, and he gave the head nod and stopped to talk to us.

Yes, he actually walked over to talk to us.

I had nothing to say, to be honest. I'd used up everything when I hollered out "what's up." I managed to mumble out something like "have a good game coach" or "go get 'em" or something equally shameful. I don't remember. I just remember that when he walked away, I felt incredibly stupid.

Go get 'em? That's the best you can do in a clutch?

Sitting on my couch, or even in the stands, I have lots of things to say. Lots of perfect advice and great words of sportsy wisdom. Intricate analysis that every professional player and coach must be dying to hear, I'm sure. I can run whole conversations through my head of what I'd say to someone, a legend in my own mind. And then the actual real-life moment comes, and all I have is a mumbled "go get 'em."

We are all seriously flawed people.

Fabulously flawed, actually, but you can only think of it that way when you realize (with great relief) that God doesn't have a ranking system.

His Word is full of verses that tell us how much He loves us despite those flaws. In fact, if I were to try to collect all those verses for you, I would eventually just hand you the whole Bible. My favorite verse, however, is Romans 5:8, which states the whole conundrum of our flaws and His love so perfectly. In that verse, we learn that while we were yet sinners, God still shows His love for us through Christ's death for our sins.

All your flaws, known even better than you know them, and He still died for you.

Sometimes, you think you're not so bad, and then a moment happens when it's all on the line and you can't pretend anymore and you realize you're full of flaws, including your foolish assumption that you weren't that flawed at all—even then, Christ still died for you.

As a kid, I could not comprehend this.

Sure, I read and memorized the Bible verses, and I knew the concepts and could parrot back answers. And I believed it, to be sure. But I couldn't fully *comprehend* the scope of it. Unlike God, I had a ranking system for sins. I was chasing perfection.

I would obey my parents. I wouldn't lie, not even those little ones to stretch the truth. When I heard someone cuss or use bad language, I'd outwardly be polite but think to myself that there was another person going straight to hell. In my sin ranking system, some cuss words were worse than others. Lying was a one-star sin, while cussing (depending on the word) was a two- or three-star sin.

Don't even get me started on what I thought about people who listened to anything but Christian music. And then of course, you got to the really big sins, like premarital sex or alcohol or pornography. These were 10-star sins (or higher!). Was there any hope for someone who did such things?

This was my understanding as a kid.

You'll be happy to know I've come a long way in my thinking since my childhood, and much of it has to do with being grateful, over the years, of how God has forgiven me. I've had to personally confront my addictive personality through food and pornography. The older I get, the more I am glad I'm not God and that I'm not the judge. I don't have to hand out black stars to people committing various sins. I don't have to try to figure out their heart based on their exterior. I can be friends with people who might like to drink alcohol. I don't have to hold on to a scale for rating sins and people accordingly.

While we were sinners, Christ still went ahead and died for us. Whether you're a one-star sinner or a 10-plus-star sinner, Christ went to the cross for you.

> *He didn't ask us
> to be perfect.*

He didn't wait until we got rid of a few of those stars and improved our rating.

He didn't ask us to clean up our act first.

He didn't ask us to be perfect.

He was perfect and sinless and went ahead and took care of what we couldn't do ourselves. That gift of salvation and forgiveness doesn't give me a license to sin. When my friend Todd gave me the precious gift of access to the stadium and players, I didn't spit on that gift. I didn't show up and embarrass and humiliate Todd by acting like a rude fool. I accepted and treasured the gift.

Christ gave us a perfect, precious gift, one beyond comparison to anything, but people either reject it, or too often they treat it carelessly by thinking it gives them license to sin. Or maybe they miss the grace and love that gift is wrapped in and instead allow a fear of imperfection to paralyze them. Sometimes, it's easier to point out others flaws instead of dealing with the reality of our own.

Being Flawed Is Not a Spectator Sport

Back when I was a kid, when we still read actual paper newspapers, I'd pull out the sports section and eagerly read the articles about my favorite players. You could read their stats, about the latest game, and also about their lives through their own words. I'll never forget when Johnny Manziel ("Johnny Football") came on the scene. To this day, he's still my favorite player to come through Texas A&M.

His freshman year, he set the world on fire. He was an amazing athlete and so fun to watch. His numbers rivaled the best, and he went on to win the Heisman. But there weren't too many articles about him in the newspaper that first year—not the kind I wanted to read—because the head coach at the time had a rule that didn't allow freshmen to interview with the media.

The following year, that changed. Lots of interviews and articles came out.

Eventually, we'd go on to learn a lot about Johnny Football, about who he was and what he did. In all honesty, the closer we got to him and the more we got to know about him and his flaws, the more I wished I didn't have the access. He had his own struggles he was working through, like anyone, but when someone is a celebrity, we paint a picture in our minds of perfection, and those flaws cause some cognitive dissonance. We see this more today with social media because we have so much access to famous people, even though it's often controlled through a PR firm or a brand image or filters that try to hide the flaws. They don't want us to see their flaws, and they find a way to give their fans more access without seeing the imperfection.

"Look at me, look at me, but don't look too closely!" is basically the rule of the internet. We learn to set aside what's real and try to believe what isn't.

I find it beyond weird that my girls will spend more hours watching people on YouTube opening toys and playing with them rather than playing with their own toys. Some adults do the same kind of thing, watching real people living their life on TV instead of shutting the TV off and living their own life. We're entranced by the illusion of perfection, by the heightened dramatic flaws, and our own real life seems to pale in comparison. Not only are we imperfect in comparison, but our flaws aren't even as dramatic!

God made us for a purpose, but we'd rather be spectators of other's lives and maybe sit on our couch and judge them on our scale of perfection and sin instead of doing the hard work of living our own flawed lives ourselves.

I still love Johnny Football, flaws and all.

God loves us, flaws and all. And if you believe there is beauty in the broken, you'll start to see that you're not flawed, you're *fabulously* flawed. We have to stop seeing perfection as the only source of beauty, the only thing of value or worth saving. We can't slap an Instagram filter on our lives. If we were perfect, we wouldn't need Jesus. Jesus, who was perfection, gave His life to save sinners, not perfect people. God believed those sinners, with all of their flaws, had incredible value worth saving.

I understand the frustration that comes from living in imperfection. I tell you, there are so many things in my life that I have wrestled with and sought counsel for, and here I am, still contending and fighting. My desire is to please God, and my flaws frustrate me. Even the apostle Paul understood this struggle, and he writes in Romans 7:19 that there is good he wants to do, but the evil he doesn't want to do is what he keeps on doing.

It's very hard to believe God can love us like this. One morning, I was listening to the song "Jireh" by Maverick City Music, and the lyrics really gripped my heart.

"I'll never be more loved than I am right now . . ." the song goes, making the point that I don't have to win a trophy to make God proud, to make Him love me any more than He does in that moment, that being a sinner with flaws wasn't letting Him down.

Our sins and flaws don't catch God by surprise. He knows, and often better than we do ourselves. While I used to get so bothered and angry when I failed because I wanted to please God to show Him how grateful I am for what He's done for me, I see now how that was keeping me from the calling He placed on my life.

Our sins and flaws don't catch God by surprise.

God didn't call me to be perfect. He doesn't expect me to achieve perfection before I can step out in what He's called me to do. And if I'm paralyzed because I can't get past how I'm not good enough to do what He's asking of me, to live in the passion he placed in my heart, that's a problem. It was only when I really took hold of how much He loves me in spite of my flaws that I finally found the freedom and confidence to step out in faith. I could stop being a spectator of other's lives and get out on the field and live the life He had planned for me.

Over the years, I've gotten to meet a lot of really cool people. I've also gotten to meet a few not-so-cool people. There was this one dude who was like a living piece of self-Velcro. He was so stuck on himself at a nauseating level. We could be talking about anything under the sun, and he'd find a way to bring the conversation back to him.

People like that aren't difficult just because they're so self-focused; they're also difficult because that self-focus skews how they see every-one else. That meant he was quick to talk about others (and by others, I mean a lot of people I respected and liked), telling me of their flaws and how he was able to "save the day" in a situation where they clearly dropped the ball.

I liked the guy and even respected him to some degree, but this aspect of him was incredibly distasteful and confusing. In one instance, I'd see God using him to literally reach and change thousands of lives for the better, and the next moment, the self-centered person would emerge.

I was so puzzled by this, but over the years, I've met a lot of people with huge influences that were incredibly flawed. Some had such an amazing outward ministry, but I'd go out of my way to avoid interacting with them personally, or I'd have to pray through before I worked with them. I had to brace for what was coming.

But isn't that encouraging in a weird way? God uses flawed, flawed people. He puts priceless treasure in jars of clay like me and like you.[12] He doesn't save his greatest works for perfect people; He uses the flawed people. Though it can still be confusing, once I began seeing these kinds of people from this perspective, it helped me pursue my own calling. It helped free me from the bondage of chasing perfection.

---

12   2 Corinthians 4:7.

You Can Chase Perfection, But You Won't Catch It

There is an inverse relationship between chasing perfection and being perfect.

I have discovered that truth over all the years I spent chasing perfection. Trying to be perfect, or waiting for perfection to arrive, only increased at an astronomical rate the gap between me and that elusive perfection. In the 1989 movie *National Lampoon's Christmas Vacation*, we learn that Cousin Eddie, a fellow wallowing in many, many flaws, has made that mistake. While his family has lost their home and is forced to live in a sketchy RV running on gas fumes, he isn't doing much to help their financial situation.

"In seven years, he couldn't find a job?" Clark asks his wife Ellen, concerned that Eddie's kids wouldn't have Christmas gifts.

"Catherine says he's been holding out for a management position," she replies.

Are you holding out for perfection?

Psalm 23 is a beautiful and well-known passage. If you've ever attended church (or a funeral), you've probably heard it. *The Message: The Bible in Contemporary Language* paraphrases it so well, though, making its meaning all the more rich:

> *God, my shepherd! I don't need a thing. You have bedded me down in lush meadows, you find me quiet pools to drink from. True to your word, you let me catch my breath and send me in the right direction.*
>
> *Even when the way goes through Death Valley, I'm not afraid when you walk at my side.*
>
> *Your trusty shepherd's crook makes me feel secure.*
>
> *You serve me a six-course dinner right in front of my enemies. You revive my drooping head; my cup brims with blessing.*
>
> *Your beauty and love chase after me every day of my life. I'm back home in the house of God for the rest of my life.*

It's a picture of God taking great care of us, above and beyond, in all our imperfections. When I'm walking through Death Valley, I don't have to be afraid. I don't have to be brought down by the devil, who is all too happy to remind me of all my faults and flaws, hoping I'll believe him when he says I deserve to be in Death Valley because I'm so broken. Instead, just like security guards left me alone in that stadium as long as Todd was with me, Jesus is there.

"Hey," He says to the devil. "He's with me."

The devil scurries off.

When I choked in front of the running backs coach and barely managed a "go get 'em," my friend Todd was still with me, and I got to continue through the stadium and still experience that amazing day. I didn't have to be smooth and eloquent and perfect. I just had to be with Todd. And in life, especially in Death Valley, it's exactly the same—I just have to walk it with Jesus. Even if I'm stumbling, Jesus doesn't leave me.

One of the saddest things is how many people who never drank or smoked or swore will still be filling hell. Some might have even been baptized or confirmed. They might have been recognized as an important person in the community, someone who helped neighbors and was honest and reliable and always did kind things. They appeared close to perfect, but they weren't walking with Jesus.

Either people are sitting around, waiting for everything to be perfect; or they're aggressively trying to perfect themselves in their own power. The first one won't walk with Jesus because they never see themselves better than the sum of their flaws; the second one won't walk with Jesus because they think they can earn His love instead of just receiving it as a gift.

Both fall short of the mark.

And in a way, both are based on a kind of fear. Fear to admit you're loved by God because that means your life has value and is meant to be lived accordingly. Fear to admit you can't do it on your own, so you set out to prove your own strength and skill to the world.

Fear paralyzes people. There's a reason perfect love casts out fear, according to 1 John 4:18. Fear often masquerades as anger and hate, but when you get right down to most of the things that destroy, it's all about fear.

Fear of missing out, of being alone, of being hurt. Fear of doing the wrong thing, of being shamed. Fear of being at fault or failing. Fear of change or fear of never being changed. Fear from the past, and fear of the unknown. Every so often, a documentary comes out that terrifies people. Whether it has the message that their drinking water is toxic or their food is killing them, those kinds of documentaries have the power to create paralyzing fear in people, even though it might be veiled as anger for a righteous cause.

I get it. Fear kept me at a standstill for years. But I've had to come to a place where I take the experiences and information I come across, prayerfully consider it, and then make the changes that are needed as best I can—all while not walking in fear. My hope and trust are in the Lord. I don't have the understanding nor the ability to comprehend and control everything. Only God can, so I will leave that to Him and follow His lead for the rest.

> ## *Fear kept me at a standstill for years.*

You don't have to be foolish and ignore useful information, but the enemy would like nothing more than to use anything he can to wrap you up in chains of fear. Sometimes useful information for one person can be bondage for another. The stress, tension, and anxiety that's eating up our culture today come from this spirit of fear that the enemy has cast over the world.

Think of it this way: imagine you were specifically created and meant for greatness, and in spite of flaws and failures, that would never change. Imagine the level of freedom you would have!

You don't have to imagine that because it's true!

That's how it is with God. In fact, when you take a wander through the pages of Scripture, you find that God often bypasses the religious folks, those trying to achieve perfection through their own works, and ends up using incredibly broken and flawed people instead.

Jacob was a cheater. Peter had a temper and was overzealous and might cut off your ear. David had an affair, and then had the woman's husband killed. Noah built the ark against all odds, and then after that was all over, he got drunk and passed out naked. Jonah ran from God and was upset when God showed mercy to his enemies. Paul was a murderer. Gideon was fearful and insecure. Miriam was a gossiper. Martha was a worry wart. Thomas doubted. Sara was impatient. Elijah was moody. Moses stuttered and murdered. Zacchaeus was physically short and disliked as a tax collector. Abraham was old. Lazarus was dead. Jesus was perfect, and they murdered Him.

Peter is one of my favorites. He managed to fight when he shouldn't, and he cowered when he should've stood strong. Peter had faith to hop out of the boat and walk on the water toward Jesus, but the fear caused his faith to waver so that he began to sink. In Matthew 16, we see Peter correctly identifying Jesus as the Messiah and getting praise from Jesus in verses 17 and 18, but by verse 23, Jesus had said to him, "Get behind me, Satan! You are a stumbling block to me."

God used Peter mightily. By Acts 5, after Pentecost when the church had been established, we see a different Peter, one whose very shadow healed people through the power of God. By the time Peter died, he had written two books in the New Testament.

I'm grateful for the flaws.

Paul wrote about this beautifully in 2 Corinthians 12:1–12. I like the *Message* paraphrase of this passage:

> *You've forced me to talk this way, and I do it against my better judgment. But now that we're at it, I may as well bring up the matter of visions and revelations that God gave me. For instance, I know a man who, fourteen years ago, was seized by Christ and swept in ecstasy to the heights of heaven. I really don't know if this took place in the body or out of it; only God knows. I also know that this man was hijacked into paradise—again, whether in or out of the body, I don't know; God knows. There he heard the unspeakable spoken, but was forbidden to tell what he heard. This is the man I want to talk about. But about myself, I'm not saying another word apart from the humiliations.*
>
> *If I had a mind to brag a little, I could probably do it without looking ridiculous, and I'd still be speaking plain truth all the way. But I'll spare you. I don't want anyone imagining me as anything*

other than the fool you'd encounter if you saw me on the street or heard me talk.

Because of the extravagance of those revelations, and so I wouldn't get a big head, I was given the gift of a handicap to keep me in constant touch with my limitations. Satan's angel did his best to get me down; what he in fact did was push me to my knees. No danger then of walking around high and mighty! At first I didn't think of it as a gift, and begged God to remove it. Three times I did that, and then he told me,

My grace is enough; it's all you need.

My strength comes into its own in your weakness.

I need that passage in my Bible so much. It has helped me quit focusing on the flaws, and instead appreciate the gift. Christ's strength is revealed in my weakness. God receives glory when He enables me to do His work despite my failures. It's not me doing anything; it's clearly God at work.

Now I take limitations in stride, and with a pretty good attitude, because those limitations keep me humble and give God more room to work and shine. Abuse, accidents, opposition, bad breaks—I just let Christ take over! In Christ, there is an inverse relationship between strength and weakness. In Him, the weaker I get, the stronger I become.

Do you want to God to use you to bring Him glory?

Do you want to fulfill your purpose?

You'll never be perfect, so set that aside. Instead, take your steps forward with God now instead of waiting for a "better" time. If you wait until you're good enough, you'll be one of those really nice people who end up in hell because they didn't walk with Jesus. Without Him, even our very best moments and attempts at goodness and righteousness are like filthy rags.[13]

His grace is enough. Stop focusing on your flaws and focus on Jesus's flawlessness. He loves you, and His love is perfect because God is love.

During a Disney cruise, my girls and I were standing in line, waiting to meet Mickey Mouse. Suddenly, from the back of the line, there came a commotion. All of the repressed anticipation of kids and parents waiting

13   *Isaiah 64:6.*

in line for so long bubbled up and out as cameras flashed and Mickey Mouse walked into the room. My girls' faces were priceless.

Despite the initial excitement, the line was long, and so Tiffany took the girls to get a snack while I held our place. I began to do a little people watching, observing those around me as they had their turn with Mickey Mouse.

All walks of life were there, waiting to get a photo with Mickey Mouse. A sweet old lady with a walker. A girl in a wheelchair. Some people were dressed in expensive clothes, and others looked like they had sneaked aboard like Jack on the *Titanic*. Kids and adults alike of every possible ethnic group, Mickey Mouse patiently treated them with kindness. Rich or poor, young or old, black or white, walking or in a wheelchair, Mickey greeted everyone with a hop in his step, and he laughed and hugged.

This is like seeing Jesus in Mickey ears, I thought.

In John 13:34–35, Jesus tells us that we are to love one another, following His example, and that the way we loved others is how people would know we were His followers. It frustrates me how sometimes Christians, who have as many flaws as anyone else, can't seem to even mimic Mickey Mouse, much less Jesus. There are a lot of hurting people out there (ourselves included), and you know how the saying goes: hurt people *hurt* people.

But what if we loved?

We can focus on our flaws, find them frustrating or disgusting, and turn that fear and anger toward others. Or we can love. Be generous with people. Be kind right out of the gate, making it your go-to mode of interacting with everyone. Just that simple act of choosing to live focused on Jesus, enjoying your walk with Him despite your flaws, and learning to love other people is how you move toward that greatness God intended.

We have two dogs, and one, named Luka, is a sheepadoodle. He's young but huge and getting even huger. It's ridiculous how large he is. Yet as a puppy, he got used to a little pen we kept him in that was in the kitchen. He's big enough now to get out of it easily, but because he grew up in that little pen, he's unaware of what he's capable of. He stays in the pen.

Don't stay in the pen you're in. Don't let fear or flaws keep you from stepping out. Jesus saved you, and you are destined for more than staying in a pen and trying to be perfect there.

CHAPTER 11

I AM, Right Now!

A few years ago, we faced another difficult time of testing. From the outside, I'm sure it looked like things were going well and that life was perfect for us. Our company was doing well financially. Our health was on point. Our kids were happy, and Payton was as healthy as she had ever been. Everything was in place, and we felt like the time was right to take our dream vacation.

We'd put a lot of thought into that vacation because we don't always get to travel with Payton. As I said earlier, it is so difficult and complex to do. Stepping into her bedroom is like stepping into a hospital room, though we've camouflaged it well for her using bright colors to make it a happy place. But that kind of medical care is hard to take on vacation. Will we be able to take her nurses? Can we get her medical equipment there? Are we outside of flu season? Is she in good enough health?

We worked hard to check all of these boxes, and we decided on a dream Disney cruise. We'd taken her to Disney once on her Make-A-Wish trip and learned that, if Payton gets upset and is ready to lay down for the day, that day is over for all of us. She calls the shots. We thought that on a cruise ship, she could still get the Disney experience of meeting the characters, but also be back at her room any time she wanted.

We were able to rent the necessary health equipment and have it sent to the cruise line. We had two nurses go with us. Everything was looking up, and off to the cruise we went.

One night, there was a themed pirate night. We decided to go all in because in our family, we just don't do anything halfway. Be warned that if you hang out with us, it's all or nothing, so buckle up, buttercup! Anyway, all five of us were in pirate gear. I did the whole Johnny Depp Jack Sparrow costume with a wig, eyeliner, and everything. It must have been pretty good as far as costumes go, because people were coming up to me to ask for a photo. Perhaps they didn't know I was just some guy from room 5216.

After dinner, the girls wanted to go look at the toys in one of the stores on the ship. There were some Mickey Mouse pirate ships that caught their eye, so Disney isn't dumb when it comes to marketing. Parker wanted to take her ship back to the room early so she could play with it, and I volunteered to go with her because—I'm not going to lie—being Jack Sparrow was a sweaty ordeal. Wearing a heavy pirate coat on a cruise ship in July is a good way to drop fifty pounds in water weight, fast.

Back in the room, I told Parker to let me get my costume off first, and then I'd be out there to help her open the box. A few minutes later, I came back to the room and saw her holding her eye.

She wasn't crying, but I could feel panic and something heavy in the room.

"What's wrong?" I asked, rushing over to her.

She wouldn't answer, and she wouldn't let me look at her eye.

What had happened was, while I was changing, she tried to open the box herself. The box slipped out of her hand and the corner of it jabbed her in the eye. Soon, she began crying and grabbing at me because the panic had now settled in.

I felt incredibly helpless. Here we were, in the middle of nowhere with an injury, and I couldn't even reach Tiff because of the lack of a signal for a phone. All I could do was pray for my baby girl. And pray we did. We prayed and prayed.

"I can't see, daddy!" she kept saying. "It's blurry!"

The longer it went on, the more anxious I became. I couldn't tell how bad her eye was, but I was very concerned. We still had four days left on the cruise, and I didn't know what we'd do. Would they have to fly her home? Would they stop in some random port in a country with sketchy hospitals and just leave us there? I had no idea, but I knew she needed help, and Tiffany would be gone for hours because they'd gone to see the show and fireworks on the top deck.

We were both crying and praying, but she agreed to try and rest and laid down on her bed. When Tiffany finally got back, I told her what had happened. We got both girls to bed and covered them both in prayer.

The next morning, Parker still couldn't see clearly. We went to the onboard doctor, and while she was concerned, they only had limited equipment onboard. The best she could offer was a recommendation that we go to an eye specialist the day we got back. We tried to enjoy the rest of the trip with our princesses, but I'll admit I found it difficult not to worry. Our dream vacation seemed to drag on forever.

Me and Parker.

Once we got back home, we went straight to a specialist. He confirmed the worst, informing us that Parker had a significant cut on her eye. There are three layers that make up the eye, and the pirate ship box had penetrated the first two.

"If it had gone one more centimeter, it would have hit her retina," he said. At her age, that would have left her permanently blind in her left eye. Thankfully, they were able to perform emergency surgery to replace her lens and stitch up the deep cut. To this day, you can't tell what happened unless you catch the sparkle the sun makes on her new lens.

Maybe this sounds like nothing big, particularly in light of what we'd gone through with Payton. But it was a moment where we were supposedly on the mountaintop, having our perfect dream vacation, before quickly plunging into a valley where worry and fear got a grip. Life is full of those crazy ups and downs, but even in the middle of nowhere out on the ocean, God was present. We weren't alone. He was still faithful; He stopped that box that night and spared Parker from partial blindness.

At The Mercy of The Wave

Perfection is overrated. (You may have picked up on my thoughts on that in the last chapter.) Daily commitment is what is priceless. But I have to confess that I just about scrapped this whole book right near the finish

Life is full of those crazy ups and downs, but even in the middle of nowhere out on the ocean, God was present.

line. Made it through the first ten chapters, and then I had a bad couple of weeks; and that was nearly enough for me to call it quits. Then, in the midst of what was going on, I read John 11:35 (*The Message*).

"You don't have to wait for the End. I am, right now, Resurrection and Life," Jesus told Martha, who was brokenhearted because her brother Lazarus had died and she was grasping at the hope of his resurrection someday, at the end of the age.

Tiff and I love to travel. We love seeing new places or visiting the ones we've seen on TV. The experiences that come with travel have value to us. We've both gone through a lot, losing loved ones and dreams, and we have come to the place where making memories is far more valuable than owning possessions. If given the chance between getting a gift or making a memory, we'd choose the memory every time.

Reading John 11:35 got me thinking about some of the trips we'd been on, including that dream Disney cruise. How foolish would it have been to wait until the trip was over to celebrate and enjoy it? Plodding through the trip and then, after pulling into the driveway and unloading the bags, turning to each other and slapping a high-five and cheering at last for all the things we'd experienced. That's not how it's done. My girls are so excited the night before a trip, they can hardly sleep. That's before we even start it, much less all that happens during it.

We have to remember that we aren't promised tomorrow and that we need to make the most of each day. So many of us, myself included, live for the mountaintop experience. Yet we aren't meant to live on mountaintops. Life can't be sustained above the tree line. It's hard to breathe, food is scarce, the soil is shallow, and very few plants or shrubs can live there. While the views from the top are incredible and can energize and inspire you, growth comes in the valley.

Life is a lot like that.

We all take our bumps and bruises along the way, those things we call growing pains that are part of growing up. The beauty in the broken is that we are able to learn so much in that valley, more than we ever could from the mountaintop. Up high, we get a broad view, but it lacks detail. In the valley, we see much more in a different way.

While writing this chapter, I watched a documentary on surfers who were chasing the perfect wave. They were looking for one hundred-foot waves found near Hawaii, South Africa, Australia, and Portugal and figuring out how to surf them. Many had dedicated their whole lives and life savings to finding this wave and had even lost friends along the way due to surfing accidents.

In the film, I watched as they were pulled out by Jet Skis and dropped off right in front of these massive waves. The Jet Ski would frantically get out of there, and those dudes would try and ride these colossal acts of God. It was incredible to watch, but I had to think how crazy you have to be to risk everything to try that kind of wave. But to them, this wasn't everything; this was just the journey. It was what they did every day. It was what they loved.

If you've ever been in the ocean and felt the power of a one- or two-foot wave, and how such a small wave can make you look pretty stupid if you're not paying attention, imagine those giant waves. What would a one hundred-foot waves feel like? One of the surfers described it by saying that after you're knocked off your board, you're at the mercy of the waves. You don't move your arms or legs because the power is just too much, and you'll break something if you try. You get knocked under the water and hope your last breath was enough to get you through because you'll be under for a few minutes. You lose all sense of direction, and it gets dark. You're scared to move, but you know you can get really hurt in the crash of the wave.

So, there I was, in the two weeks of being in the valley, when I thought I'd just give up on writing this book. How is it that you can start writing a book and even have a chapter where you're shouting from the mountaintops that God has helped you work through depression and find that you've tumbled back into the valley?

I'm writing a book to give hope to others, to inspire them, and now I'm down again! I thought. Was I a hypocrite? Did I start the book too soon? Should I have waited until I'd "arrived" and all of that was behind me?

And so, I stopped at chapter 10 because I'd lost direction and ended up in a dark place. Over eight doctor appointments for my mom, watching her—my spiritual giant—struggle with vascular dementia. Having the same conversations over and over when I drive her to the doctor. She thinks the car we sold years ago has been stolen. She calls me by my dad's name. I know it's not her fault, but add that to the mix of all the craziness of the pandemic and all the pro/anti groups and the politics and the geopolitical nightmares springing up everywhere and the devastating earthquakes and disasters that seem to happen every day, and then the unexpected death of a young man who was in the youth group I pastored—I was falling into a serious funk. I was struggling to put one foot in front of the other; my spirit was so heavy.

It felt like the world was on fire, and I was drowning in a massive wave of despair.

But then, after taking my mom to a doctor appointment and pulling into the driveway of her assisted living home, she turned to me.

"I don't know why, honey, but I've had this song on my heart all day," she said to me, and she began singing the old hymn "I Feel Like Traveling On." We used to sing that song a lot in their church when I was growing up.

My heavenly home is bright and fair, I feel like traveling on.

"I wish I could repay you for taking me to all of these appointments," she said, her independent spirit as strong as ever.

Nor pain, nor death can enter there, I feel like traveling on.

"Could I pray for you?" she asked me. I've always coveted my mom's prayers, and I quickly agreed.

Let others seek a home below, I feel like traveling on.

Which flames devour or waves o'erflow, I feel like traveling on.

My mother prayed. And, as always, she spoke with such clarity and power. It felt like Heaven came down into that car, and a sense of peace took root in my heart. My story wasn't going to stop at chapter 10 after all. I knew I would start the next chapter that night.

Speaking of chapter 11, let's go back to chapter 11 in the book of John.

When You're in a Dark Place

Mary, Martha, and Lazarus, all siblings, had a special place in Jesus's heart. They were His close friends, and He loved that family. Mary is the one who used expensive oils to clean and massage His feet, even using her hair to wipe them down.

In John 11, we learn that Lazarus had become very sick, and someone sent word to Jesus.

"Lord, the one you love is sick," He was told, but He stayed two more days where He was so He could continue ministering. Then He told his disciples it was time to head back to Judea, to where Lazarus was.

"Our friend Lazarus has fallen asleep," Jesus told them. "I have to go wake him up."

"If he's sick, wouldn't it be better for him to sleep?" the disciples wondered. They didn't understand what was going on, so Jesus told them that Lazarus had died.

"I'm glad I wasn't there, because this is a chance to display God's power and help you believe," Jesus said.

When they arrived, Mary stayed in the house, but Martha ran out to meet them. "Why weren't you here?" she cried.

I get how she feels. I think you do, too. *Lord, don't you care? Have you forgotten about me? Am I even a blip on Your radar? I thought You loved me! I thought we were close! Why did You let this happen?!*

> ## He is resurrection and life; we don't have to wait for the end to have joy.

I'm so glad God is patient with us. There are times I should have been shut off. I can't imagine what it's like to hear that from people all day, every day, as if He wasn't faithfully present always. But instead of cutting us off or pushing us away, He pulls us in even closer.

"Martha, your brother will rise again," Jesus told her.

"I know he will rise again in the resurrection, on the last day," she said. I can picture her, weeping and confused, a mixture of sadness and anger and love and hope.

And then Jesus said the most amazing thing, that verse I shared earlier. "You don't have to wait for the End. I am, right now, Resurrection and Life."

I LOVE THAT! I love that so much! I AM, right now! Resurrection and Life! He's with us right now. He is resurrection and life; we don't have to wait for the end to have joy.

Then, Jesus asked where they put Lazarus's body, and they led him to the tomb. And then the most incredible thing happened: Jesus fell and wept.

John 11:35 is the shortest verse in the Bible, simply telling us that Jesus wept. How powerful that is! I know you, like myself, have gone through some tough stuff, and it's broken us down. And even though God is all-powerful and all-knowing and knows the outcome of it all . . . He still weeps for you and with you. He's not oblivious to your pain, even when He knows what good will come from it.

Jesus told them to move the stone.

"Lazarus has been dead for four days. He's going to stink," they told him. That's gritty realism right there.

But Jesus already knew what would happen, and so they moved the stone.

"Lazarus!" He called out. "Let's go!"

Lazarus was in a very dark place; he was buried in a tomb. He was as done as done can be.

That was how I felt during those weeks when I just about gave up, when I felt alone and in a funk by choice. I say by choice because we choose who we partner with. Tiffany could tell something was eating away at me, and she even reached out to my good friend and life coach Dave, but I didn't want to talk to anyone. I just felt done. I'd come this far but felt like God couldn't use me.

I don't know how to write a book. I can't tell someone how to hang onto hope when I can't do it myself. I don't feel any hope right now. Those thoughts went over and over in my head.

Dead, in a tomb of despair. That was where I was.

But I can tell you that God never left me. He was there the whole time, and He was patient with me. Tiff was patient with me. And just like Jesus wept for Lazarus, even though He knew the good ending, I think He wept with me.

Every time we go through something that seems bigger than us, heavier than us—even if we can't exactly put words to what is eating away at us—God is with us. We don't see what He sees. When Tiff and I were so broke, we couldn't see beyond it. When we were sick and unhealthy, we didn't see the Spartan and half-marathon runners He saw.

We can't hold onto mountaintop experiences, where we think we finally see everything. We can't get to the top and plant ourselves there. We have to keep going, even when there's a valley coming. Valleys can be hard to get out of, and mountaintops can be tough to leave. But God is with us and wants us to keep moving one step at a time.

When I trained for the Spartan, I worked my way up to running six miles at a time. I didn't pull that off in my first day of training. I just wanted to run for a minute without stopping. It was hard, but I kept building up without thinking about running the full six miles.

I've never run six miles, I'd think as I gasped for breath, *but I can run for one more minute.*

Then, I'd block everything out and try to run for just a minute. And then I'd do it again. And again.

When I finally showed up for the Spartan, I was so intimidated. I saw myself as a 345-pound man with severe health problems and more self-doubt than you could imagine. When the race started, I was surprised. It was just like I'd practiced. It was just like I'd run before.

Can I do it for a minute? For another minute? Another minute? I didn't try to think about finishing all twenty-three obstacles. I just tried to finish the one in front of me. Jump over the wall, run another minute. Climb the rope, run another minute.

When I was done, I was scratched and beat-up and sore beyond belief. But crossing that finish line was exhilarating. I'm glad I didn't have a high mountaintop view of the course before I started; I don't know how that would have messed with my mind. From my ground view, one step and one minute at a time, I could do it. Mountaintops are like God's wink to you, a moment to get up at the top with Him, allowing that happiness to pause and reflect at where you've come and where both of you are going next—but you can't stay there.

At a recent men's conference we had at our church, the Christian band Leeland performed a new song they'd written. The lead singer introduced it by talking about Yahweh, another name for God. He talked about how the very name means breath of God, and that even when you breathe, you are crying out to God—the very sound is yahhh-weeehhh, yahhh-weehhhh.

No matter how hard life gets, no matter how dark things are, just take a deep breath and cry out to Yahweh. Take it one breath at a time, and God will be with you and use you to do great things.

How do you finish a Spartan? One step at a time.

How do you get out of weeks of depression? One day at a time, God at your side.

How do you call out to God? One breath at a time.

Shortly after the men's conference, Zachary, one of our worship pastors, was leading during Sunday morning church. He paused, and then shared that his name meant "God remembers."

"I just wanted you to know that God remembers you," he said.

It was as if I was hearing the word "remember" for the first time. When we think of the word "remember," we usually think of memories. But, if you break down the word, it means re-members. He mends or puts you back together again. He re-members you, making you whole.

You are not forgotten.

You are not broken, but if you feel that way, God re-members.

Don't try to rush to the finish line.

Remind yourself that I AM is right now.

That's a good list to hold on to, but sometimes it's hard to know how to live it practically. I've found the following actions helpful:

Make time daily for God, because otherwise, you get busy, you quickly forget God is there with you, and the relationship grows cold.

Surround yourself with people who make you better. If you don't work out, start; the endorphins will make you feel better.

Read and listen to things that fuel your goals, and if you don't have a goal, set one.

Most of all, fall in love with the journey.

When you fall in love with these kinds of action steps, bit by bit, you get to your milestone, and you'll love what you're doing every day. If you don't love what you're doing every day, mountaintops will always lead to letdowns and setbacks because you dread the journey into the valleys.

*Don't try to rush to
the finish line.
Remind yourself that
I AM is right now.*

As I worked my way out of that dark place of depression, I met with my coach, Dave. He is such a lifesaver to me and my family, and once again, he hit on what was bothering me. In the midst of all the horrors happening in the world and the personal struggles in my family, I was feeling guilt.

"It's OK to be blessed," he told me. Sometimes, I struggle with that, oddly. He then asked a series of questions, and one jumped out at me. "Are you tired of needing permission to dream and create your dreams?" he asked.

We worked very hard to break the chains oppressing our family (and for generations to come), and God blessed us. But still, I have held myself hostage because of that amazing life we've created for ourselves. Without realizing it, I am still comparing people myself to other people and still asking the same question I asked many years ago from our very different lives.

God, why me?

First, I questioned why God had us in the valley, then I questioned why he had us on a mountaintop. It felt like I didn't deserve either; and in both cases, I chose to let dark feelings take over because I forgot the great I AM was with me.

Do you forget that He's with you? If that's you, I want to pray for you.

God, I lift up whoever is reading this right now. You see and know what they are facing. Maybe they feel like they're out in the middle of the ocean with no help around, or that they reached a goal and are disappointed that it didn't feel better. Whatever it is, You see what's weighing them down. You promised that Your yoke is easy and Your burden light, because You are a good Father. I know You'll carry the heavy stuff for us. So, Yahweh, please breathe life into them. Let them feel the very hope and peace that can only come from You. If you need to resurrect some dreams, we ask You to speak life into them. In Jesus's name, amen.

CHAPTER 12

When Words Don't Come Easy

Back in the day, I was much more confident. Maybe it was because I still had hair. Maybe it was because I was in a band, and that made me cool.

Granted, our band got to play at the Lightspot, a Christian club and hangout in Kaufman, Texas, where bands like Skillet and Switchfoot and Bleach played. Some of their cool probably rubbed off on us. The owner of the club wanted to create a place where teens could safely hang out, and he'd bring in all kinds of amazing Christian bands. We might not have been as cool as the O.C. Supertones, but we got our chance on the stage.

In fact, we weren't the only local band to play the stage. My personal favorite band was a local one called The Shake, and I'm sure there are still restraining orders out on me from the guys in that band. Due largely to those guys (and perhaps to their dismay), music had such a huge part in shaping my life. To this day, when I need a little therapy or calming down, I pick up my acoustic guitar or sit at the piano and just play music. When Payton gets upset or uneasy, music has a calming effect on her, too. Worship and singing have gotten me through a lot of hard days.

The Lightspot was very popular, and after our set one evening, I was back at the table to help sell our band's merch. I glanced down the line of people, and my eyes fell on the most gorgeous blonde woman I'd ever seen. She had the greenest eyes, and she took my breath away. I later found out that she was wearing colored contacts, but that didn't matter.

What did matter was that she wanted one of our 8x10 band photos, but she only had forty-seven cents. Those bad boys were a dollar, but she was hot, and forty-seven seemed close enough. The whole band signed it for her, and that was how I learned her name was Tiffany.

The joke was on her, really, because I'd printed those photos out the night before on my color printer, and they weren't even worth forty-seven cents. And maybe the joke was on both of us because we were different people then. I often wonder what would have happened if the Tiff I know today and the Andy I contend with today would have met. I don't think I would have been able to ask her out, but that doesn't matter now. God knew. He ordered our steps. He brought us together and knew we needed each other.

Forty-seven cents, a scribbled autograph, and I met my future wife. What a concert!

Many months later—or maybe it was years, I can't remember, which is why guys get in trouble when anniversaries roll around—Tiffany came to a music festival with our youth group. She still had those green eyes, was as gorgeous and amazing as ever, and we spent over twelve hours in the 100-plus-degree July Texas heat. I figured if she was still into me after spending a day with me at my sweatiest and stinkiest, she was a keeper. I mean, she even laughed at my jokes back then. I'm not sure if she was being nice or if I've forgotten how to be funny since then and stumbled into dad humor, but it amazes me to think about it. I knew that day that I would spend the rest of my life with her.

Me and Tiffany on our honeymoon, so young with no clue what was ahead for us.

I'm talking lightly here, but I'm about to get into something pretty serious.

We have to talk about marriage; we've talked about nearly everything else, so I think you knew this was coming. This book is about sharing hope to those in need of hope, and when it comes to marriage, we've all heard the stats. We've heard the numbers. Marriages are under attack, couples are hurting, and families are being split apart.

Right now, as I'm writing this, I have close friends fighting for their marriage.

I have another friend, a dude who means the world to me, who just served his wife with divorce papers. He wasn't flippant about it but had spent years fighting and seeking Godly counsel, and the day came. I've had three close family members affected by divorce.

What I'm trying to say is that this topic hits close to home and painfully so, for everyone, including me. I've gone back and forth debating whether to even talk about this in the book, whether it's worth including when I run the risk of offending or opening the wounds of people I care about.

Let me start by saying that I just want to have a conversation with you. Whether your marriage is a perfect 10 or on the last moments of life support, or whether you've already lost your marriage or haven't been married yet, my prayer is that something in this chapter will speak to you. I've prayed, given it to God, and trust that He'll use the words I'm putting on the page. I'm praying that He'll surround you with peace and comfort and that He'll use my words to build you up, encourage you, and lead you to healing.

If you feel like you're at the end of your rope, God has something he wants you to know.

The Third Strand

As much as I love my football and sports and armchair coaching, as much as I love to cheer and holler and revel in the thrill of a close game, I'm going to let you in on a deep dark secret: I really love weddings.

(I'll wait a moment so you can pick the book up off the floor.)

Not everyone feels the same way. I've heard it said that the difference between a wedding and a funeral is that at a funeral, at least one person is at peace. I completely disagree; weddings are awesome.

My brother and his new wife had a wedding that we hosted at our house. It was such a beautiful ceremony, one where you could feel the presence of the Lord so strong at the service. I couldn't help but think—through watery eyes I was trying hard to hide—how powerful weddings are because two become one. Unfortunately, for many people, weddings have so much stress leading up to them that we basically miss the actual wedding moment and meaning.

At my brother's wedding, I was asked to pray a blessing over them at the end of the ceremony. I don't remember everything, but I do remember feeling the Holy Spirit prodding me to say something in particular.

"Lord," I prayed out loud, "we invited you to be here at the wedding, and now we invite you to be in this marriage."

Two become one. In Ecclesiastes 4:12 (*The Message*), we learn that by ourselves, we are unprotected. "With a friend, you can face the worst. Can you round up a third? A three-stranded rope isn't easily snapped," the Scripture says.

When you're alone, you're unprotected. At first read, when I was thinking about this Scripture, I thought the obvious understanding of that verse was that the first strand was you and the second was the spouse. But bummer for the single person.

"No, dummy," I felt the Lord say (no, I don't think He called me dummy, but it wouldn't have been out of line at the moment). "You don't have to be married to have Me in your life."

The protector is God. He tells us in Proverbs 18:24 that He is a friend who sticks closer than a brother. So, by yourself you're unprotected, but with your friend, you can face the worst. That's you and God. That's His promise to us.

What if the third strand is our spouse? A three-stranded rope isn't easily snapped.

Boom.

The dream team, right there.

That's where we first miss the boat, putting so much hope and pressure on our spouse, a burden they weren't ever intended to carry. That part belongs to the Lord. He's the protector strand. He's the one who promises to never leave or forsake us. We go together like peanut butter and jelly, beans and rice, milk and cookies, peas and carrots, bacon and . . . everything.

The bottom line is: our hope in life is put in Jesus and not our spouse. We do that first. After that, what if we find that third strand? That's a tough piece of rope! What could break it? Well, if the rope starts to unravel itself from within, breaking it becomes easier. The rope can break itself, and we do it all the time.

My coach, Dave, is so good at simplifying things and making them practical for me, and one of the things he's shared with me so many times is that we have to lay down the right to be right.

Picture this scene: the morning started out just fine. Sun came up, there was breakfast, and the day commenced. By evening, however, it's a full-on rumble. You're fighting with your spouse about something completely stupid, like old food in the fridge or dirty socks on the floor or neglecting to take out the garbage or a lost house key. It's all stuff that doesn't matter, but you've made it matter; and both of you are going for broke to win the fight. It's amazing how a disagreement about something trivial can become the Greatest Hits of All the Wrong Things You Ever Did, isn't it?

In the midst of that fight, with words pouring out of your mouth that you'll absolutely regret, you wonder how you got there. I know Tiffany and I have wondered that. Some of our fights are so silly, it's embarrassing. If only we could learn to surrender the right to be right and avoid going down a path of fighting.

For example, I'm a details person; I think details are important. Tiffany thinks details are optional. Which one of us is right? That's the wrong question, but it's the one we ask. Instead of understanding that our Creator chose to make us different so our lives weren't boring, we want to fight about which one is right.

Tiffany might be telling a story. It's a wild, wonderful story, and she has everyone at the edge of their chair. But I'm listening and thinking, *Huh, those numbers don't add up* or *Those details aren't correct* or *That's not logically possible.*

I feel the need to step in and help clean up the story, and that's when I get the look.

THE LOOK.

You know what I'm talking about.

Sometimes, it's a growl. It depends on how bad my interruption was.

This is so hard for me. All I can see are details, and I can't grasp how Tiffany sees a big picture with an eye for emotional impact. It's like interrupting a guy telling a hilarious fish story to correct him on the lure he used or to debate the true size of the fish. I'm working at getting better on this, and when we're both surrendering in this area of needing to be right, we end up enjoying each other's company a lot more. You can apply this principle to just about any relationship in your life.

Take friendships, for example. What would your best friend think if suddenly, one day, you just laid down the need to be right? Would the friendship improve? Would your friend be so surprised that you'd need to resuscitate them? But that example is easy enough; best friends are worth the effort, just like a spouse. So, let's up the ante.

What if you applied this principle on social media?

I know there are some who are possibly searching for me on Facebook right now, getting ready to leave a comment like "enjoyed your new book, but you have some ideological errors in chapter 12 . . ." Social media brings out the worst in most of us. If you're a people-watcher like I am, the only thing better than doing that in person is going on social media and watching strangers have a fight in the comments section. I can't begin to calculate the amount of time I've wasted watching Joemama67242 insist on one thing, then joker247 chimes in and says, "no, you're wrong," then gifmaster8429 starts dumping rude memes in the mix. Pretty soon the time-space continuum is broken, and time stops as all things revolve around their online flame war. I know you've gotten sucked into that, too, lurking and simultaneously talking to God about how they need Jesus while pharisaically being thankful you're not like them, even while you secretly can't wait to see who responds next.

Seriously, this world is so jacked up right now that families are separating over a silly social media post because someone needs to be right. Is it really worth it? Is it worth damaging your witness as a follower of Christ because you had to win an argument online? Most of us have a conscience that's convicting the life out of us on that one, so let's move on.

What if you laid down your right to be right in your relationship with God?

What if you laid down your right to be right in your relationship with God?

Oh, yes, when asked in Sunday school, you'll tell the world that God is all-knowing and all-powerful and has the whole world in His hands, but in private, you spend a lot of time trying to convince God you're right.

"Lord, I really think it would be better if this problem were solved this way. I know You created the world and everything in it in six days, but just check out my ideas. I think You missed this."

Over and over in the Bible, we see God asking us for obedience. I don't mean to burst your bubble, but He could probably find someone more talented to do whatever it is that He's asking you to do. What He's doing is giving you an opportunity to grow and partner with Him if you'll do it the way He's asking. What if you replaced all your but-God's with here-I-am's instead and see where your spiritual journey would take you? What if you partnered with Him instead of trying to unravel His strand from the rope?

When Words Don't Come Easy

My brothers wrote songs for their wives on their wedding days, so I just assumed that was what everyone did. I'm now aware it's not, and having heard people sing karaoke, I think that's OK. But I wanted to do a song for my wedding, and so I set about writing a song for Tiffany.

The music came pretty easy. The key, the chords—it all flowed. But unless I was going to just hum the tune or try to romance my future wife with scat singing, I had a problem. I could not figure out the lyrics. The words weren't coming to me, no matter how hard I tried. I had this general idea of what I wanted to convey; but when the words fell out onto the paper, they were horrible. It didn't make great sense.

A few weeks before the wedding, my future mother-in-law called me. "Son, we need the name of your song. We're putting it in the wedding program."

Uh. Um. My mind raced, and finally I blurted out, "When Words Don't Come Easy!"

I'd named my song after my struggle, and now I was committed to it. But the words just started spilling out from there, and I finished the song that day. I had no idea what was in store for Tiff and me; and when I look back, I can see how prophetic the song was for what our marriage would be like.

When words don't come easy,
I'll live to please thee,
with every breath of my life.

I thank God for the blessings,
that He gives me.
For my beautiful wife.

And if the rain should fall,
Or if tragedy calls,
And our back's against the wall.

I'll be there, I'll show you I care.
You can count on me.
When words don't come easy.
When your heart breaks,
Or your Earth quakes girl,
You can believe.
I'll live to please thee.
When words don't come easy.

So, when stress catches up to us
Or you're feeling emotionless
I'll be by your side.

If my words leave you hurting
I promise I won't desert thee,
This you can't deny.

So, if you've had a bad day,
And I don't know what to say.
Let my actions lead the way.

I'll be there, I'll show you I care.
You can count on me.
When words don't come easy.
When your heart breaks,
Or your Earth quakes girl,
You can believe.

I'll live to please thee.
When words don't come easy.

And so, as time passes us by.
I'll consider myself the luckiest guy . . .

To be there, to show you I care.
To have you count on me.
When words don't come easy.
When your heart breaks,
Or your Earth quakes girl,
You can believe.
I'll live to please thee.
When words don't come easy.

> *Marriage is the most selfless thing you can do because it's not about you.*

Three months later, we got a surprise phone call that my uncle, who was at the wedding, died suddenly from a massive heart attack. He was way too young, and he had a huge influence on my life and thousands of others. And of course, you know all the other things that happened in our lives and how soon after our marriage Tiffany would lose her parents.

But the promise remains true.

I promised I'd be there, good or bad. We made the choice on our wedding day that divorce was not an option. We're far, far from perfect, but we try to be better every single day.

Marriage is the most selfless thing you can do because it's not about you. If you're selfish, if you're looking at the other person as being there to meet your needs and solve your problems and be what you want them to be, you're going to struggle in your marriage. Tiffany and I are a team. In our business, in our family, in everything we do, we're a team. If she loses, I lose. When she wins, I win. We're not playing solo.

One of the things I love about baseball is the promise of a new season. When spring rolls around, every team feels like they're going to win it all. But it's such a long season that, somewhere along the way, teams lose that hope. For some teams, it only takes a week or two before they know (and boy, if that's your favorite team, that's a horrible season). Some make it halfway through before they know. Others make it to the final few weeks of the year before they're eliminated from the playoffs.

Marriage is much more complicated than baseball season. I feel like we start relationships off on impossible ground, that we're dating our PR firms. We only let the other person see the best of us, not the real us. The other spouse has no idea of the baggage that's coming on board. Just like a brand-new baseball season, we jump into marriage thinking our team is going to win it all; but somewhere along the way, we lose focus. Division creeps in, hope withers, and slowly, we separate. No one gets married with the goal of divorce.

I've seen the devastating splatter pattern of divorce firsthand. As a youth pastor, I saw so many kids' lives wrecked because mom and dad chose to go separate ways. I'm not judging you if you're coming from a failed marriage; my heart goes out to you because I've seen the devastation it also does in the spouse. It's bad all around, a kind of death. It's the death of a hope and a dream; but unlike other deaths where there's a funeral and a body you can see and lay to rest, mourning a divorce can go on and on. How do you bury a dream? Who understands?

But if we don't look at ourselves and what we brought into the marriage that broke up that three-stranded rope from within, we'll go on to the next relationship with the same baggage and the same ending.

Helping others with marriages over the years, I've noticed a few common factors. While I'm not a marriage counselor, we served as marriage ministry pastors for the last few years of our ministry at the church; and we saw a lot of broken marriages that were mended. I want to share what we observed, the most common things people contended with in their marriage.

1. **Expectations.** This is that strong belief that something specific is going to happen. Expectations aren't bad, they're neutral. They can be helpful in pursuing goals, for example. In a marriage, though, they can cause damage when there's no action behind them. Lots of fights happen when the expectation inside our mind never gets out. Women might expect their

husbands to change once they get married. A husband might expect intimacy every time, but the wife wants a few hours to relax after a long day. For most guys, every time is the perfect time, and we're ready to go. Women aren't like that. God has a great sense of humor. Unspoken expectation, and expectation without action that would lead to it, are destructive.

2. **Pursuit.** When you follow someone, you pursue them. Before I got married, I pursued Tiffany. She was into the Mavericks when we were dating and could name all of the players. Twenty years later, she only knows the name of one player, and that's because it's the same name as our dog. She gave up her pursuit. Guys also love to pursue, to hunt. We were made for it. Back in the day, food didn't come served up on a plate; we had to hunt for it. We learned that when we did the action, we'd get a predictable result. So, why do we forget that in our marriages? You want more sex, then put in your talking time, take out the trash, wash the dishes, help with the kids. That's your hunt. That's true foreplay. It's part of the pursuit. Husbands have to keep pursuing their wives, and wives have to pursue their husbands. Because here's the bad news: if you don't pursue them, someone else will.

3. **Communication.** Ah, the big C. Marriages are blown out of water by this one. When Tiffany and I both started working from home, our very first day together led to our biggest fight. I was trying to find my place in the well-oiled machine she'd been running without me while I was working outside the home. She had an efficient routine, and she also had some expectations from me. I can't remember how it started, and I don't remember the bickering in between, but it ended with Tiffany saying, "You work for me now!" Here's some free advice to the ladies: never, ever, in a million years say that to your husband. We didn't get much work done that day. I was personally lost, as I like structure; at the time, I was starting something new and trying to find a routine. Tiffany thought that when I came on board, I'd be like some of her mentors, even though we're totally different. It would probably have been a good idea to sit down and talk about this beforehand. But even now, twenty-two years into our marriage, it's tough. Women use a lot more words to describe a

situation, while we dudes try to say it with as few as possible. Again, God has a hilarious sense of humor. Hilarious.

4. **Rejection.** Dismissing a person, an idea, a proposal, or a gesture hurts, especially for men. The toughest dude is shaken to the core by rejection, especially if you're like me and wear a self-esteem button right on your chest. It's easy to take rejection personally, especially if communication isn't well-established. I once had expectations of how I thought the night would go, but then Tiffany would say no; and so I'd find a "safer" avenue to pursue what I thought I needed, someplace I wouldn't get rejected. I got it so twisted that I thought I was doing her a favor by watching pornography, but I quickly learned that sin only serves to separate. It separated me from God, and it separated me from Tiffany. I was shattering Tiffany's self-esteem and trust, rejecting her for the image on the screen. This might sound strange, but plan for intimacy. Schedule it. Your wife can prepare mentally for it, and you can add time for a massage to relax if needed. I know it sounds very un-Hollywood, but it's better than walking a tightrope of bad communication and anger over rejection. Wives, if it's not going to happen, let your husband know that tonight might not be the night so he doesn't feel rejected later. Guys, don't think in terms of basketball, but instead, think baseball. Keep swinging for the fences. Thirty percent would be a horrible free throw percentage but would make you a Hall of Famer if you had that average in baseball.

5. **Grace.** Grace is something that's incredibly generous, totally unexpected, and totally undeserved. None of us are perfect; we're all human, and we all mess up. That doesn't give us permission to sin or treat our spouse poorly, but it does mean that we let each other down from time to time. We should work to view our spouse the way God does! Instead of seeing all their flaws and keeping a list of all the things they've done wrong, you'll see them in pure love. God offered the gift of grace to us, and now we offer that same free gift to our spouse.

You know that amazing song I wrote for Tiffany, when I made all those promises at the beginning of our "season" of marriage?

I haven't always lived up to it.

I haven't always been there or shown her that I care. In fact, many times *I* was the very reason why words didn't come easy. I love the three-stranded rope analogy so much because that's where God comes in. He is our anchor.

Imagine marriage as one of those crazy roller coasters, the kind where you're strapped into a hanging chair, suspended from the track above you. The longer you've been married, the easier it is to imagine this scene.

Anyway, think of God as the rollercoaster. He's the main cog in your marriage. He has a firm grip on you. He's on one side, your spouse is on the other. While it's a wild ride, with new heights and plunging lows, as long as all three of you stay connected, you'll make it.

I look back at the journey Tiffany and I have been on, and I am in awe. As I write this, we're in Hawaii for work, and I'm on the balcony listening to the waves come in. Wave after wave after wave. They never stop. They're faithful to keep washing up on the shore.

God is faithful; the Bible tells us this over and over. He is faithful like the rising of the sun every morning and the rising of the moon every evening. His mercies are new every day. You can count on Him. Follow in His faithfulness and give your spouse a new day with a new start each morning. Be like those waves, rolling in love and forgiveness day after day.

I was praying about the best advice I could give for marriages, and it came down to each spouse connecting with God like never before. John 3:30 says that God must increase, and we must decrease. In *The Message*, it's described as God moving to the center while we slip off to the sidelines.

Build your marriage around Jesus. Keep Him at the center. Keep that three-stranded rope tight. Don't allow sin and the enemy to eat away at it from within.

Now and then along the journey with your partners, you'll be like me, sitting on a balcony, listening to the ocean, remembering the past twenty-two years and all the ups and downs God has brought you through, and you'll think: "Wow, what a ride!"

Terrifying, exhilarating, full of screams and laughter—and all worth it.

Don't Look Back

Looking back is easier. I meet a lot of people who find it easier to look back than to dream and move forward. It's easier to mull over the past than imagine a future.

I drove my little princesses to school one day, and one of them spoke up. "Daddy, play that workout song you like," she said. Clearly, this was a moment for Survivor's 1982 "Eye of the Tiger."

I pulled that song up on my music app, and we started rockin' and air guitarin', and a flood of emotions and memories came over me. I told them about *Rocky*, the best movie series of all time. I told them I could remember exactly where I was the first time I saw *Rocky* and even the first time I heard "Eye of the Tiger."

Later that weekend, I sat down to watch the Rangers play the White Sox, who were wearing their throwback uniforms, white with the black and red stripe across their chest and the word sox across it. That took me back to my childhood; everything from my childhood was just better, and I guess that officially makes me old. I could see Harold Baines and the original pudge Carlton Fisk. All the guys I hadn't thought about in nearly thirty years until I saw those uniforms.

Music does the same thing. When Aerosmith's "I Don't Want to Miss a Thing" comes on, I remember what movie theater I was at. When I hear Bryan Adams's "Everything I Do," I remember that wonderful moment when I found out it was cool for guys to wear tights. Even certain smells and sounds can take me back, like the scent of burnt popcorn, or the sound of shoes squeaking on a gym floor.

I know I'm not alone in this. Nostalgia and a resurgence of "retro" wannabe 1980s TV shows and movies tell me others can understand. Looking back is easier because it's safe. There are no surprises because we already know what happened. For most of us, the memories that come back are of happy times because we hold onto good memories. In our pasts, we were carefree.

I was riding with my friend Barrett the other day after church. He asked me a simple question during that short drive, one that rocked my world.

"Did you ever think you would be here, writing a book?"

I laughed. "No way, dude."

This echoed an earlier experience. I'd been texting Pastor Judy, the wife and co-pastor of a church we served in ministry for many years. She'd wanted to see a few chapters of the book, and I shared some with her. She responded, speaking into my life and addressing some of those underlying self-esteem issues I have.

"Andy," she texted, "you totally amaze me! You're deep and pensive. I see that as wisdom. I want you to see yourself as a writer, because you are one."

My safety net was to tell people I was *trying* to write a book but that I didn't know what I was doing. It was my way of saying, "Hey, you read the book despite my warning. I told you I didn't know what I was doing; so if you don't like it, it's not my fault."

That was to help me from getting hurt. It seemed like a win-win. But was it?

Does God want us to be walking in safety, whether we're trying to relive the past or have an excuse for every person who might say something negative about us? God wants us to walk forward in the freedom He bought for us, not run backward to safety. For me, that means I have to say to myself repeatedly that I am a writer.

While in Cape Town, South Africa, we'd just finished an incredible three-day conference, where the Lord touched many lives. I was sitting in the hotel lobby with Pat Schatzline and his assistant, Daniel. It was well past midnight, but we couldn't sleep. Just like Pastor Judy did with her text message, Pat began to speak into my life. He knew from me reaching out to him months earlier that I had gone through the wringer, and that I felt like I'd wasted so much time and wasn't fulfilling my calling. So, there in that hotel lobby, late at night, we spoke about what had happened earlier in the evening.

Pat can work a room; he has a God-given talent for connecting to people. He's a powerful communicator who lets the Lord use him. However, earlier that night, up on the stage in front of thousands, he'd handed me the mic and told me to speak life into the people who were there.

I thought he was crazy. I was terrified I'd mess it up. But he pushed me into that place where I had to fully rely on God to reach my full potential, and Pat knew that. He understood that it would be uncomfortable, but that in the long run, it would be best for me. And you know what? God didn't abandon me. He helped me that night, giving me the words to say, and my words changed lives for the better.

Recently, my daughter Presley was told by her coach the night before a game that she'd be playing goalie. My heart skipped a beat because that's a lot of pressure. I didn't tell her that, of course, but instead told her I was so proud of her. She smiled and was very excited; she'd never played goalie and was inexperienced at soccer in general. On the other hand, I was so nervous. I wanted the best for her. I told her everything I knew about being a goalie, which took about five seconds. Seriously, what do I know about soccer?

On the day of the game, she was in a different-colored jersey from the rest of the team. She got to wear the goalie gloves. She was going to play for the first half, so we only had twenty minutes before this was all over. I'm certain I was more nervous than she was, but she took on the challenge like a champ. The game started, and the action picked up quickly.

Presley playing goalie.

First save, no problem. Second save bounced off her shoulder and out of bounds. That one shook her up a little bit, but she was OK. Then, the momentum swung, and the opposing team started getting goals. Each time, I saw the disappointment on her face, and I so badly wanted to run out there to help her. I could see it—daddy-daughter tandem goalie. I was ready to go full-on Billy Madison because I hated seeing the disappointment. I also hated hearing the things people sitting around us were saying. But she never gave up, even when she missed a block. Afterward, we got some ice cream and headed to church. It ended up being a fantastic day, and she was all smiles. I was proud of her not because of the score on the board, but because she stepped up to the challenge.

Safety doesn't move forward; it becomes a crutch in a lot of different ways. We avoid what's difficult. We sit back and just get nailed with what's coming instead of stepping up to meet the challenge. We live in the past and dwell on past victories or failures.

Did you know that the difference between an amateur golfer and a professional golfer is about 1.5 strokes each hole? That doesn't seem like much, but it adds up quickly, ending up to about 27 strokes on an 18-hole course. If we could focus on getting better and looking at what's next instead of feeling sorry for ourselves because of what's current, we could make a huge difference with just tiny changes.

What has God called you to do? What is your passion?

The biggest obstacle to fulfilling His calling is confrontation. We don't want to confront what scares us, so we'll accept a mediocre way of living. We stick with the life we're used to. I remember after losing the weight, going from 345 to a lanky 185, how much I wanted to put on muscle. So, I confronted my fear of the gym and the "real" bodybuilders and did the work. I still get a body scan the first of every month because it doesn't lie; it tells me if I've put in the work or not. Confronting your fears and reaching your goals isn't a one-and-done; it's a process.

So, what are your goals? Have you thought about it, or is it easier to think back to old memories and dwell in safety rather than make new ones? In Genesis, we read the story of Lot's wife. It's not a very long story, unfortunately, because against God's orders, she chose to look back at what she'd left behind and was turned to a pillar of salt. She never got past her past.

Maybe it seems too far-fetched or impossible, but couldn't you take small steps, one day at a time? Couldn't you make changes and take even small actions that are aligned with your goal?

Consider that if I were to go out and buy a baseball, it would cost about six bucks. So, in my hands, a Major League Baseball is worth only six bucks. But in the hands of Mike Trout, that same baseball is worth a cool $340 million. There was a point, though, where that ball was only worth six bucks when Trout held it. Sometime, back when he was younger, he began the work to become the baseball player he is today. I imagine there were times when he wanted to quit or didn't believe he and his team would get where they are today. When I watch him play now, it only makes me want to get better.

What gift do you have in your hands? What will you do with it? Will you share it with the world, or hide and protect it and hope you don't lose it? I love the story of the talents in Matthew 25:14–30. It tells of a wealthy man going off on a long trip. He delegates responsibilities to his servants. One servant is given $5,000, another is given $2,000, and another $1,000, all based on their abilities. Then, he left on his trip.

The first servant immediately set about doubling his master's investment, as did the second servant. But the fellow with only $1,000 decided to dig a hole and bury his master's money.

When the wealthy man came back from his trip, he called his servants in to settle up. The first servant showed how he'd turned $5,000 into $10,000.

"Good work!" the wealthy man said. "You did a great job, and from now on, I'd like you to be my partner."

The second servant was next, and he showed how he had also doubled what had been given to him, presenting the full $4,000.

"Good work!" the wealthy man said. "You did a great job, and from now on, I'd like you to be my partner."

The last servant came forward. He must have been feeling a little nervous at this point. "Master, I know you have high standards, can be pretty tough and demanding, and don't like people to be careless. There didn't seem to be any room for error." The man paused, and then went on. "I was afraid to disappoint you, so I found a good hiding place and hid your money. It was safe and sound, and here—you have it all back, down to the last penny."

The wealthy man was furious at the servant. "If you know I demanded the best, why did you do less than the minimum effort possible? You could have at least put the money in a bank and I could have earned a little interest from it!"

The wealthy man then demanded that the $1,000 be taken from that servant and given to the servant who had risked the most. "Get rid of this servant, who will only live cautiously. Throw him out into the darkness."

That's a paraphrase of the parable, but it's sobering nonetheless. For years, I played it safe. I was scared into living cautiously.

I wanted to be stronger but didn't want to go to a gym.

I wanted to be a leader but didn't want to lead.

I wanted to write a book to tell my story but was paralyzed in fear about what people might think of it.

God has called you to greatness! Whether you're at a $5,000 or a $2,000 level, I don't know, but I do know that how much work you put into it matters and that sitting back and playing it safe is not an option. The exhilaration comes from slaying goals and getting to the finish line after a hard battle, not looking back and living in memories.

So, here it is, the end of my first book.

I had doubts this day would come, but I persevered in the race and I made it—and it feels incredible! One day, I'll finish the race of life, and more than anything, I want to stand up in front of my Lord and tell Him I did my absolute best with the talents and opportunities He gave me.

I wasn't sure anyone would care to read my story; but you, like me, are writing your life's story in a blank journal, one day at a time. My desire is for my story to give you hope, to encourage you. Revelation 12:11 tells us how important our testimony is, and that when we partner with Jesus and show how He is woven into our lives, our testimony can be part of how we overcome.

My story is one of brokenness upon brokenness, and yet it's also a story of incredible beauty. That only happens because Jesus is present in every page of my story, whether I realized it or not.

What's your story? Are you writing in your life's journal today, or are you spending your time reading yesterday's entry? Each day is a blank page, and you have a chance to change the ending, but only if you can see there is beauty in what's broken and are willing to keep moving forward.

Acknowledgements

First, I'd like to thank my Lord and Savior Jesus Christ for partnering with me to deliver this message of hope. I pray that the words used in this book bring glory to You and serve to help everyone who reads it.

To my dear friend Dave Blanchard, CEO of the Og Mandino group. Thank you for the countless hours on Zoom and on the phone. It's been an honor working on this project with you. You pulled out the best in me, and I will appreciate you forever, friend.

To my new friends at Story Chorus (Jordan, Anna, Ashton, and Jackson). I just wanted to thank all of you for taking this dream of mine and turning it into a reality. You took my baby and treated it with kid gloves. I'm so grateful for all of your hard work and dedication to this project. None of this would have been possible without you, and I thank you so much!

To baby P, Paypay (Payton). Baby girl, I love you so much. You've pushed me more than you'll ever know. I bet if I know your momma well, she's reading this to you right now, and I can see your face lighting up with the smile that melts the hardest of hearts. Your story is literally reaching millions, just like we used to pray for. Wow! I love you so much. I long for the day we can sit back and have our own conversation, our own slow dance without the wheelchair, share laughs together, and hear your story from your mouth. But until then, I will always be reminded of the beauty in the broken. I love you, baby girl!

To Park Park (Parker). You are growing up so fast! I want you to always know I love you fiercely. I am so proud of you. You'll never know the role you and your sister played in my restoration. It was an answered prayer with a cherry on top when we found out we were having twins. God is faithful. Promise me you'll never forget the faithfulness and closeness of our loving Father. I can't wait to see what He does with your soft and loving heart. You care about people so strongly, and it will serve you well in life. Stay close to the Father, and don't be afraid to listen to His call. I love you, baby girl!

To Prey Prey (Presley). Oh, Presley, I love you so much, baby girl! I was the baby, too. I know you're only the baby by two minutes, but we will always have that common ground. I am so proud of you. Just like your sisters, you have your own calling on your life. Every day, I see you growing and blossoming so fast. Like your sister, you'll never know the impact or role you played in my healing. Gosh, I still remember it like it was yesterday, you walking around the kitchen in a diaper and your baby walker, just babbling as you walked. You've always been a talker. You get that from your momma, but those big feet come from your daddy. I love how you always have the courage to take on huge challenges, even when most people wouldn't. You are never afraid to step up. I love you, baby girl. I can't wait to see what God does with your life and all your creative gifts!

To all my close friends and family. You know who you are; every single one of you that I do life with. I wouldn't be here without your encouragement, wisdom, shoulders to cry on, inspirational pep talks, all of it! I can't mention names here because I would never forgive myself if I left someone out. Just know you, (insert your name here), are loved, and I appreciate you more than you'll ever know.

And last, but definitely not least, my bride Tiffany! Wow, what a ride, huh? We had no clue what we were getting into when we said "I do." What do we do when words don't come easy? We just keep going. I love you! I am so stinkin' proud of you and all your accomplishments. People often push me to the side just to get to you, and I understand why. I've been pushing people to the side for almost twenty-three years now just to get to you, too. I love watching you work in your passion and seeing you inspire and motivate millions of people. I've had the best seat in the house for this journey, and I wouldn't change a thing. To quote Garth (you know a country bumpkin like myself has to quote Garth): "And now, I'm glad I didn't know, the way it all would end, the way it all would go. Our lives are better left to chance, I could have missed the pain, but I'd have had to miss the dance."

I look forward to seeing where God takes us every year, month, day, step, and breath. I'm grateful for every moment I get to share with you. Thank you for your never-ending support, for holding me when I couldn't hold myself together, and for being an advocate for Payton when I couldn't. I love you so much!

About the Author

For over twenty years, Andy Howard has served in ministry as a youth pastor and marriage ministry pastor. He has found that not much changes in each role, just that some come with more wrinkles and less hair.

Andy is an advocate for mental health awareness as he has known the heaviness of depression himself. He is passionate about fighting against the awful attack of mental health issues that are running rampant across the human race.

At his heaviest Andy weighed 345 lbs and his wife Tiffany weighed 317 lbs. Together, they have lost over 350 lbs combined and have co-founded a health coaching business called *Taking Back My Life* where they have helped thousands of people get healthy as well. Through this journey, Andy has become passionate about fitness and working out.

Andy loves traveling and sharing his and his family's story with churches, conferences, and youth camps. In his spare time, he enjoys following his favorite sports teams and shooting zombies on Playstation (you probably didn't see that coming).

Andy was born in Bryan, Texas and currently lives outside Dallas, TX with his wife Tiffany and their three beautiful daughters Payton, Parker, and Presley.

Find Andy on Facebook and Instagram @AndyBHoward.